OUT
OF THE
GATE

WHAT THOUGHT LEADERS ARE SAYING ABOUT
OUT OF THE GATE

"*Out of the Gate* is very thought provoking. Henrietta Pepper's collection of self-disclosing stories truly causes you to examine the same subjects from your own history and perspective. It inspires you to reflect on similar times and how they impacted your life and you as a person. The author's roots in Kentucky provide the perfect backdrop to the Thoroughbred racing and horse-country themes throughout the book. Ultimately, the stories will motivate you to push to the finish line in a healthy mind, body, and spirit style through all phases of life."

—LORI AND TIM LAIRD, Authors of
That's Entertaining! with Tim Laird, That's Entertaining! Cocktails and Appetizers,
and recently released *The Bourbon Country Cookbook: New Southern Entertaining:*
95 Recipes and More from a Modern Kentucky Kitchen featuring David Danielson,
Executive Chef at Churchill Downs, the home of the Kentucky Derby

"Henrietta's reflective writing style and honest approach takes the power of story-telling one step further to story-sharing, which challenges the reader to reflect on their own experiences while inspiring new ideas and offering insights to discovering purpose. Her authentic, compelling stories are a breath of fresh air. I'm reminded that what we experience in life, good and bad, should be embraced, appreciated and remembered. Our story is what makes each of us unique and this book is a compilation of stories that remind us to share, connect and inspire . . . always."

—BELINDA GATES, Author of *Your Successful Life:*
The Playbook for Defining and Achieving What Success Means to You,
Compass Enterprise, LLC Executive Coaching,
and Leadership Development Wildside Institute, Founder

"I often found myself laughing out loud (and shedding an occasional tear) as I read *Out of the Gate*. Henrietta has a way of storytelling that makes the reader feel they are right in the room with her, experiencing the joy, the sorrow, or the humor of life. The various life tales will leave you reflecting on your own story and what sort of legacy you want to leave for your family and friends. Some nuggets of wisdom that will leave you thinking that just maybe you can make a difference!"

—**MARY VARGA**, Author of *The Light Through My Tunnel: Overcoming Tragedy Through Courage & Faith* and *The Afflicted Healer: With Mind, Body & Spirit Guest Authors,* Founder & Owner of SilverStrength® Senior Fitness

"So many times in life we experience hardship and feel alone while walking that path. Henrietta does a masterful job sharing her life experiences, letting you know that you are "not alone." All the while, reassuring you that you can and will get through these tough times. You can feel her unvarnished honesty in every page, and her attention to detail keeps you on the edge of your seat for the next story!"

—**ROB KING III**, Northwestern Mutual, Financial Advisor

"Kern's Kitchen and its famous Derby-Pie® dessert brand are built around stories centered on family values, work ethic and ingenuity spanning over 60 years. In her professional career, Henrietta has helped clients, like our company, elevate their brands through compelling storytelling.

Out of the Gate takes her abilities to craft and share stories to a deeper personal level. Every reader should be able to identify with these stories that may tug at your heart and/or challenge your perspective on life. The unique flow of the stories does a great job of balancing those dynamics throughout the book."

—**ALAN RUPP**, Kern's Kitchen, President

What inspires us drives us forward.

OUT
OF THE
GATE

Powerful Stories of Faith, Family, and Friends.

Henrietta Pepper

IGNITE PRESS
Fresno, CA

Published in the United States by Ignite Press.
IgnitePress.us

ISBN: 978-1-950710-86-7 (Amazon Print)
ISBN: 978-1-950710-87-4 (IngramSpark) PAPERBACK
ISBN: 978-1-950710-89-8 (IngramSpark) HARDCOVER
ISBN: 978-1-950710-90-4 (Smashwords)

For bulk purchase and for booking, contact:

Henrietta Pepper
OutOfTheGateBook.com
OutOfTheGateBook@gmail.com

Library of Congress Control Number: 2020916862

Edited by White Arrow Editorial Services LLC
Interior design by Evolve Layout Services

DEDICATION

I dedicate this story-sharing experience to my husband of thirty years.
Larry, this isn't our first time going down a path of new adventures. As usual, you were my rock and my biggest supporter. You kept me going during the tough times and celebrated the joyous milestones. It has been a journey filled with a lot of laughs and sprinkled with some tears along the way.

There is one thing that this time has crystalized for us both. God is in control and continues to bless us dearly. Thank you for being by my side. My love, forever.

ACKNOWLEDGEMENTS

When I started down the path of authoring a book, I had no idea how much planning, expertise and just good, old-fashioned "attagirl" nods of support it would take to get it over the finish line.

To my husband, Larry, and our amazing kids (and their spouses) and grandkids: *There were alot of times I thought about giving up this idea of sharing a part of our lives. I'm glad you kept my feet to the fire. My heart is full. I can't wait to see what the next seasons bring our family. Good thing there is power in numbers!*

To my parents and siblings: *Thanks for inspiring so many of the stories that celebrate the cherished memories we share. I love you.*

To my beloved St. James' Episcopal Church parish and choir family: *Thanks for your caring and nurturing, even through the most difficult of times. God has united us to be stronger than ever.*

To Backside Learning Center at Churchill Downs: *Thanks for the empowering work that you do for equine workers and their families. I am so honored to dedicate a portion of the book proceeds to such a resourceful organization.*

To the numerous individuals and organizations who worked alongside me during the last eighteen months:

Thank you for putting up with my whims, ever-changing aspirations, and the middle-of-the-night "what-ifs."

Cathy Fyock, The Business Book Strategist
Donna Barton Brothers
Ginger Wilding Cloud
Guardian Owl Digital Boutique
Ignite Press
Kern's Kitchen
Laura Whitus
Mary Varga
Splendid Events
The NAWBO Kentucky GROW Program's "Strive" Group
The BG Girls Beach Getaway Group
Tim and Lori Laird
Tish Kelsey

CONTENTS

FOREWORD

Let's face it, life is messy. Sure, we all **try** to be graceful and make it look effortless, but the fact remains that life is full of unforeseen challenges and we do the best we can to navigate through it all.

Henrietta Pepper creates a brilliant analogy when comparing the smooth or treacherous conditions of life to the track conditions at a Thoroughbred racetrack. There is an *unofficial* track condition I suggested as an addition: "cuppy."

A cuppy track is one that is difficult to get a hold of for the horses. It's a too-dry track that "cups" away from horse's hooves (like trying to run through dry sand on a beach), and with each stride they endeavor to find firmer footing only to have the surface slip away from them again.

As a former jockey and now horse racing reporter and analyst for NBC Sports, I can relate to all these track conditions—especially the cuppy one. And I can relate to the stories that the author poignantly relates beyond track conditions to everyday life.

There will be stories in here that resonate with you, compelling you to think, "Yes! Someone else has experienced this!" and others that might compel you to share a personal story of your own. At the end of the day, the content will make you think about your own watershed moments in life.

They will make you think about the events and people that influenced you profoundly and helped shape you into the being that you are with the beliefs that you hold. They may even convince you to examine those beliefs further and, in so doing, you may find a belief that was founded on a false premise.

The stories here will also offer fantastic conversation starters for social and/or business gatherings to break awkward moments of silence or, better yet, get that party started!

The variety of the stories are purposefully conveyed at an uneven pace. At times, the book will read fast and other times it may feel a bit "cuppy." So, just keep reading. You'll find yourself back on a fast track again soon.

There's a saying about the horse-human relationship: "Riding horses builds character." I disagree. I think riding horses *reveals* character. Only the people who want to improve their life will look at what has been revealed and then decide if they'd like to build their character. This book will offer that same opportunity. Enjoy.

DONNA BARTON BROTHERS
Award-Winning Sports Analyst and Commentator,
Author, and Former Top Jockey

INTRODUCTION

Dear Reader:

Life is complicated and we live in uncertain times. Sure, that lack of control can feel . . . frustrating. Yet it too can be quite uplifting, in a way. Sometimes that uncertainty can be a good catalyst for a mental and emotional reality check on the current state of our lives. As we navigate a blended world of family, work, friends, etc., it's easy to go through the motions without finding joy in all the little celebratory moments that are happening along the way. That is understandable. To use an analogy we're familiar with here in Kentucky's horse country: this ride called life often runs on a very sloppy track!

Life is a series of twists and turns. Good days and bad ones. Emotions are constantly and dependent upon the season of life we are experiencing. I find myself in a season of transition. As empty nesters, my husband and I downsized to another home, I sold my business, and earned an MBA at the ripe age of fifty-five.

So, while my horse is out of the gate, so to speak, I needed to push the Pause button and take stock of my life for the first time in my adulthood. I felt compelled to look in the rearview mirror to see how far I've really come. Now, I get to make new choices and direct where I'm heading next. It's been a time for reflection and lots of soul-searching. Realistically, I am mapping out my next chapter.

All of this reflecting has sparked numerous conversations and storytelling among a wide range of folks in my life. Reminiscing about our lives can be therapeutic. For me, all of this down-to-earth, honest dialogue with people who I trust has crystalized the significant role that simple life-living experiences play in our evolution. From childhood through adulthood, all of these experiences add up to a few "learning takeaways" that can be packaged in the form of a story or two.

There is such power in storytelling. The fact that we all have our own genuine tales inspired me to put my own personal stories and reflections in writing, with the intention of creating an inclusive platform for igniting ideas, provoking actions, or validating decisions.

I encourage you to take it all in through your personal lens. The snippets of life captured in this book are relatable. Be prepared to laugh out loud. Cry at the fact that life can be tough. Take deep breaths and enjoy the raw realities of it all. With that spirit in mind, I invite you to embrace, share, and most importantly, join the conversation with your own stories.

Connect at:

- outofthegatebook.com/
- outofthegatebook@gmail.com
- Out-Of-The-Gate-107504881058311/
- outofthegatebook/

SECTION 1
STAY THE COURSE

I **don't know about you**, but sometimes I get overwhelmed with life. Time seems to fly by at warp speed. Even when things are humming along smoothly, distractions pop up and we tend to get pulled in a hundred directions. When we run up on a rough patch, we try to plow through it to live another day. But isn't that just the way life rolls? We just need to do our best to roll right along with it.

It's a natural tendency to attempt to map out a well-defined, clear pathway for life. And then, life gets in the way. *If I only knew then, what I know now* is a phrase that comes to mind. Sure, there are things that I would have done differently or decisions that I would have made sooner (or later, in some cases). But when it's all said and done, isn't the best course of action to just try to *stay the course*? Life gets sloppy. There are interruptions. Yet, if we can rally around the idea of staying true to ourselves and grounded in our personal beliefs and values, navigating the seasons of life will seem more purposeful. Staying the course is tough, for certain. It's also doable and worth it—one day at a time.

SELECTED STORIES:

When Life Gets Sloppy, Pull Down Your Goggles
The Back Pew
What Is Happening?
The "I'm Sorry" Syndrome
Made of Cast Iron
Firstborn
Slow Go
Are You Really Busy, Or Are You Going Ghost?

✒ When Life Gets Sloppy, Pull Down Your Goggles

As I've mentioned earlier, Kentucky is horse country. I've found that it can be fertile ground around here for horse racing analogies around personal and professional matters. Many phrases and terminologies are tied to this "sport of kings": *get to the next turn; cross the finish line; at the starting gate; stay on the backside; hit the trifecta,* etc. I had the privilege of hearing Donna Barton Brothers, a famous female jockey, deliver the keynote at a recent symposium. Throughout her speech, it struck me how closely the *sport of horse racing* compares to the *sport of life.*

Literally, the dirt horse-track conditions and descriptions correlate with life's phases:

FAST—the track is dry, even, and resilient.

Life is good. You're humming along at a brisk, even pace.

WET FAST—a surface of water is apparent (after a heavy rain), but the base remains solid and packed down. This is still a fast surface and is often faster than a "fast" track.

You're experiencing a few issues. Maybe the pace is faster than ever. Blow-ups with your partner. Conflicts with a coworker. Your kids are giving you a hard time. Your family is displaying dysfunction. It's a heavy storm for a while; but it passes and leaves a bit of a mess to clean up.

SLOW—the surface and track base are both wet, but not evenly. This is a track that has been muddy and is now drying out and a bit inconsistent.

Life is packed down. On the surface, life might appear a little calmer; however, it is certainly not on an even keel. While some may be comfortable with this condition, it still poses inconsistencies and isn't the right pace for everyone.

GOOD—a track that is almost fast. This is a track that has been muddy, but is drying out evenly and will soon be upgraded to fast.

I believe this is the lane where we <u>attempt</u> to live our lives. We try to lead an even-keeled, disciplined lifestyle. We live on the cusp of leaping into fast-track mode, but life is still "good."

MUDDY—a wet track, but there is no standing water.

Muddy lifestyles are tricky. Because there are no real messes to clean up, you must remain intentional about your ride. How are you going to navigate life decisions? Are you going to take a risk "out of the gate" or try to finish strong at the end? Thinking objectively is critical to this part of life's game.

SLOPPY—a track that is saturated with water, and often, it's standing water.

Whether it's for a brief period or a long stretch, your life is going to get sloppy. Hold tight! The rain of disruption results in mud. Lots of sloppy mud. Just as in horse racing, mud can be blinding and painful. It can hit you in droves or tiny stings of pain. The taste of a sloppy life can be bad or good; depending on the outcome of the ride. More than anything, it can help you recognize and appreciate a FAST track that much more.

When you're on that track—get your goggles on. Pull them down as you go around the track. They will help guard you from all the grit and sludge that may come your way.

Life is stressful, and the sludge often comes at you when you least expect it. It's not a matter of IF you need the goggles; it's a question of <u>HOW MANY</u> that you have on hand when you start the race. Knowing when to pull them down is also part of the challenge. Regardless, don't go into life's ride "half-blind." Strive for a strong finish no matter how you come out of the gate. Don't let your postposition hold you back. You can always slide into another lane if that is what helps you finish ahead of the pack or, even more importantly, at a pace that works for YOU. Sometimes being first is not all it's cracked-up to be anyway.

The Back Pew

As a Christian, I am deeply rooted in my faith. I was baptized and confirmed in the Episcopal Church in Bowling Green, Kentucky. My husband and I were married at St. James' Episcopal Church in Pewee Valley, Kentucky, nearly thirty years ago. We still remain active parishioners today. I think "church" was ingrained in me at a very young age. You would find my family at the morning service almost every Sunday, wearing our designated "church" clothes. There were dresses in my closet—and then there were "church" dresses. I don't remember thinking that was odd at all. In fact, my mother will still say on occasion, "I suggest a church dress," when discussing an event.

There were unspoken rules concerning seating in church, as well. All were based on who was seated in proximity to our beloved grandmother and grandfather, "Retta" and "Big Charlie." They had two "claimed" seats in the very back pew. In fact, my extended family of aunts, uncles, and cousins were all part of the designated seating area. It was just expected to cram your family into whatever space was available. It was very close quarters at times! Where you landed depended on how early you got to the service. As little kids, the prize seat would be by Retta and Big Charlie, of course. Those are fond memories for me.

Bad behavior or "talking out" in church was not acceptable. But there were exceptions. I recall that during one of the lengthier services, my cousin asked in a loud yet unassuming voice: *When will it be over, Dad?* The entire congregation cracked up.

If you started to get squirmy, you better believe that there would be a reprimanding pinch of the arm or leg from an adult. Again, children's good behavior in church was just downright expected. You did NOT want to be taken out of church for acting up. Despite that fact, inevitably there would be the infamous unstoppable giggles in the quiet moments of the service. Even the "grown-ups" would get pulled into those awkward situations. That's just going to happen when you get that many family members in a confined space for an hour.

Occasionally, I would get a spot by my uncle who was highly spiritual and loved to sing out with gusto. However, he couldn't hit a single musical note—bless his heart. But that didn't stop him from singing from the mountaintop! Then there was the slumber. Every so often, there would be a unique snoring noise from someone in the back, usually during the sermons.

When we were older, it was considered an honor to serve in a special role during the service. These may have been as an acolyte, a choir member, or a scripture reader. My grandmother would always rave about how well her grandchildren "performed" in the service. That said, it never failed that each Sunday there would be an "incident" involving some family member. I recall my cousin and brother BOTH passing out at the altar during the summer heat when they didn't eat enough breakfast. I distinctly remember my little cousin throwing up all over his sister's new dress, which then spurred a chain reaction of vomiting throughout the family pews.

> "*It was highly important (especially to my grandmother) that we all sat together, prayed together, and even ate together after the service. I remember thinking as a teenager: Why this ritual? What's the point?*"

Indeed, Sundays were routine for our family. It was highly important (especially to my grandmother) that we all sat together, prayed together, and even ate together after the service. I remember thinking as a teenager: Why this ritual? What's the point?

Now I get it.

Sundays were a time where our family could be together; surrounded by love and embraced by God. Even though a certain level of reverence was *expected*, it taught me that God is to be *respected*, no matter where the "church" space. Over the years, I grew from *having* to go to church to *wanting* to attend services. As a teen, I was drawn to church camp and youth retreats. I branched out and started sharing my beliefs with my friends. While away at college, I continued to enjoy attending church services on campus.

"However, I realize that those Sundays in church were instrumental in forming my core spiritual beliefs"

Growing up, I didn't have near the close relationship with God that I enjoy today. However, I realize that those Sundays in church were instrumental in forming my core spiritual beliefs. Many of those beliefs weren't necessarily driven by the preaching from the pulpit. In fact, my beliefs largely emerged from the love of God and love of family that was happening near the back pew.

What Is Happening?

Flash back twenty-five years ago to the bedroom in my parents' home. Mom's newly minted two-year-old granddaughter looked fascinated as she gazed into the mirror's reflection of my mother getting dressed for the day:

"Grandma, what is happening?"

Mom told me that this was the defining moment when she realized that her fifty-plus-year-old body (at the time) was not what it was when she was in her thirties. (Years later, my mother is undoubtedly the most beautiful woman, inside and out, that you will ever meet.)

Now that I'm in my fifties, I am coming to that same realization my mom had in that moment.

It is funny how the body changes. Back in the day, I would have welcomed some extra junk in the trunk, so to speak (my kids now joke that my rear end resembles "flapjacks"). And yes, I would have enjoyed some extra fullness in my chest, like so many other women. But now, I'm *not asking for that!* Let's just be happy with our bodies and credit everything that our bodies have and will allow us to accomplish. Take care of yourself, and appreciate what God gave you.

During a recent medical exam, it was apparent I had put on some extra pounds and inches—and not necessarily in the most flattering areas. I initiated an inquiring conversation with my doctor. That weight and inches convo started with "Henrietta, give up your wine and you would drop the five pounds you hate." Now, y'all know how that's going to roll: it's not! On another front, I inquired about what this *dense breast tissue* term meant. Was that a good thing or a bad thing. What were the repercussions?

Surprise answer, ladies. My doctor replied with a completely straight face: "Well, you should look at that as a positive. Because at the end of the day, all breasts turn to fat."

> *"When I look in the mirror, I stand proud of my current look who cares if that area is fat or firm underneath those SPANX?"*

Of course, our bodies don't make or define us. It's how we project ourselves as individuals that make us each unique and special. When I look in the mirror, I stand proud of my current look—who cares if that area is fat or firm underneath those SPANX? That kind of concern is just head trash. After all, it's what's inside the *heart* that really counts.

So, I have an entirely new outlook on aging. I'm no longer ignoring the body imperfections, wrinkles, and various other signs of aging. I'm celebrating what life is all about. I'm embracing the evolution of my flesh and bones as marks of a life well lived.

> *"I'm embracing the evolution of my flesh and bones as marks of a life well lived."*

That said, I recently had my own "what is happening" moment when my three-year-old grandson looked me straight in the eye during dinner and said, "Retta, I have another grandmother that has a neck just like yours!"

I laughed till I cried.

The "I'm Sorry" Syndrome

I am making my way to the Delta Airlines terminal in Cincinnati, Ohio. For once, I had plenty of time before boarding, so I walked to the gate at a leisurely pace. Out of nowhere, a guy sprinting to his gate literally ran me over. I fell, causing me to cut my knee and rip my jeans. He did have the decency to pause and look back at me to catch my reaction. What were the first words out of my mouth? *"I'm sorry."*

> **"***Let's face it,* I'm sorry *often comes out of our mouths when there is absolutely NOTHING we need to be sorry for.***"**

What is it with women that we feel the need to say *I'm sorry* as an automatic response or lead into almost <u>anything</u> in our lives? Therapists are above my pay grade, but my theory is that it's a passive way of taking responsibility or perhaps an excuse for not changing behavior. Let's face it, *I'm sorry* often comes out of our mouths when there is absolutely NOTHING we need to be sorry for.

Are you really sorry that your friend can't find anything on the menu? When your BFF decides to go to a party instead of hanging out with you as promised? Was *I'm sorry* the only response you could muster up? Shouldn't it be the other way around?

You decide to fire Susan because she is simply not doing her job. Why the need to lead that kind of conversation with *I'm sorry—I am going to have let you go because you're not performing . . . ?*

As a parent, I found myself apologizing before applying the discipline.

"I'm sorry—I am not going to let you go in the car with an underage driver."

"I'm sorry—I am grounding you for disobeying me."

I really got good at taking blame for my kids' bold statements in a heated moment:

"I hate you right now, Mom."

"Oh honey, I'm sorry."

There's only so much time in the day that we make decisions about where that time is best spent; especially in volunteerism land. But do we really feel *sorry* about this fact?

"I'm sorry—I can't volunteer for that committee at church this year."

The worst scenarios for me tended to occur when dealing with personal relationships.

When my husband says: "I don't think we're communicating very well." It certainly doesn't deserve an immediate *I'm sorry* from me. Really!

Perhaps it's a posture of defense that allows us to absorb the blows of hurt or sadness, frustration or disappointment with two simple words.

Another example: a past serious relationship got to that phrase no one wants to hear: "I don't love you anymore."

I still regret that my first response to those hurtful words was: *I'm sorry.*

> **"*I believe this whole "I'm sorry" thing is a thing because women are nurturers and fixers by nature.*"**

I believe this whole "I'm sorry" thing is a *thing* because women are nurturers and fixers by nature. We consistently try to take on responsibility for others' unhappiness, wrong doings, or negativity. *I'm sorry* gets <u>others</u> off the hook and puts the onus on <u>us</u> for solving things.

Lately, I've been disciplining myself. Instead of an innate apologetic approach, I try to take a minute and craft a relevant, sincere reply and express an appropriate level of compassion. After all, just because I don't spontaneously apologize doesn't mean that I don't have empathy. Hopefully, needed dialogue can begin, and then I can provide guidance or help resolve a problem. Or even just be there for someone.

I'm advocating for a *Quit Saying "I'm Sorry"* movement that applies to all aspects of my human interactions. And I think that I am a much better family member, friend, and business associate because of it.

I have fallen victim to the "I'm Sorry" Syndrome in the past, but I'm just not having it anymore. And I am NOT sorry about it.

Made of Cast Iron

"My personal favorite: the sausage and milk gravy served over those homemade biscuits that only Grandma could bake from scratch"

I have very fond memories of my Grandma Pepper's cast iron skillet. It was the vessel of so many delicious Southern dishes. The iconic fried chicken resulting in just the right amount of crunch without being greasy. The straight-up perfectly cooked bacon and eggs. (No "foo-foo," fancy crepes or omelets at Grandma and Papa's house.) Fried bluegill or crappie fish was the bomb. Delicious cornbread served with sorghum or maple syrup. During special occasions, we could not wait for the freshly baked pies and cobblers. My personal favorite: the sausage and milk gravy served over those homemade biscuits that only Grandma could bake from scratch. I can't forget the infamous "coffee milk," which was 90 percent cream and sugar with a dash of coffee. Are you kidding me? Heaven.

As I would watch my grandma at work over the gas stove, the care and effort that went into cast iron cooking appeared easy and almost natural. Thinking back on those simpler of times, what was it about that singular skillet that was so magical? How does an analogy emerge to relate to the current state? I (again) went straight to the vernacular that I grew up with.

You can distill it down to how you would describe a person who is "made of cast iron." That descriptor insinuates that you perceive that individual to be rigid, strong, and unyielding. Not bad qualities to have. Digging a little deeper into the historical attributes of the amazing cast iron, I discovered some interesting factoids that are relatable to us as people who are trying to navigate these difficult times with the COVID pandemic and social unrest. We're all trying to be resolute yet approachable and comforting. Some thoughts we might want to take to heart:

her grandmother
great cook, relating/analogy to life

Even Cooking Temperature

> *"Not allowing the "elements" to get in the way and overheat in some areas and undercook in others. That requires a lot of patience and discipline . . . just like getting to that fried chicken perfection."*

This quality is one of the major advantages of the cast iron skillet. It somehow allows the food to cook evenly throughout the process: fried, baked, or simmered. Wouldn't it be wonderful if we could allow our personal inner temperaments to be on that same kind of even keel? Not allowing the "elements" to get in the way and overheat in some areas and undercook in others. That requires a lot of patience and discipline . . . just like getting to that fried chicken perfection.

Improves With Age

> *"We live. We learn. You're only going to get better as you season in life."*

Literally, every time that you cook in a cast iron pan, you are making it better by seasoning it. The more you use the surface, the smoother it becomes. When cooking in a cast iron pan, you don't need to preheat it. In other words, what you see is what you get. Relating back to what we face on the onset of each day, we can start each sunrise with an optimistic outlook, layering on to what we've already created and experienced. We live. We learn. You're only going to get better as you season in life.

Basically Indestructible

Cast iron cookware pieces are heavy and a bit cumbersome, especially in these days of light-weight cookery gadgets. Let me assure you that it is worth the extra muscle power that it takes to use the iron. The benefits outweigh the workout.

What about the cast iron's lasting power? It is difficult to ruin a cast iron pan; no matter what the make and model. So the saying "broke the mold" when describing yourself or a family member becomes descriptive and ownable.

I will gladly take on the title of "made from cast iron." After all, the cast iron skillet displays food beautifully and simply. I believe that, as God's creatures, He has given us time and talent to put forth each day. It's up to us to display it beautifully and simply. We are the vessels.

As I have expressed before, I am no Julia Childs. However, I am channeling my upbringing (which involved a lot of celebration around food and family) to better understand how I am wired and how the experiences I grew up with can be celebrated. Experiences as simple as breakfast time at Grandma's.

I believe that we are all clamoring for our inner anchors as we navigate this uncertain time and all its baggage. I suggest that we all work to be *cast iron* strong when things get tough. If that means being more compassionate, say yes. If that means making a pivot in your lifestyle to adapt and survive, do it.

Remember, *made of cast iron* means that you improve with age. Season boldly!

Firstborn

I am the firstborn in our family. I would say that I am the stereotypical eldest child: protective of my younger brother and sister, yet controlling at the same time. Growing up, I even referred to my siblings as "the kids" when speaking about them with my parents.

Many times, I found myself being protective of them, even when we would be in a disagreement. I seemed to always try to shield them from any unhappiness. And sis and bro were protective of me too. Or maybe they were just scared of me because I was the oldest.

> *"Supervising and leading people come easy; but occasionally,*
> *I find myself getting too overbearing or out of my lane when*
> *it comes to interpersonal behavior."*

That type of parental-like behavior seemed natural and intuitive to me. Even today, those instincts also carry into my professional life. Supervising and leading people come easy; but occasionally, I find myself getting too overbearing or out of my lane when it comes to interpersonal behavior. It's because I truly care about someone's well being and, again, my immediate reaction is to shepherd the flock, so to speak. I was labeled "Mother Hen" during one of my career stints for taking a "motherly" approach to leading our team through the thick-and-thin of work-life balance.

I've read several studies on the topic of birth order. I'm a believer in how that affects your personality, management style, home life, and friendships. I see this same behavior in my firstborn daughter and stepdaughter. They were acting as mini-mothers at a very young age. As my oldest daughter evolves, I encourage her to embrace her strengths and passion for life. She is a strong woman. She is expressive with her opinions, but not overbearing. What wonderful qualities to celebrate. I believe that I tried to pull back on my opinions in my young adulthood because I didn't feel it was proper to be aggressive or overt. I experienced some hard knocks in my career because of that lack of confidence. I eventually learned to hold my own in the boardroom as well as during family dinners!

> *"God has plans for us all. I guess that part of my plan was*
> *being the firstborn child."*

We are all wired differently. Each human being has a different DNA—it's unique to the individual. God has plans for us all. I guess that part of my plan was being the firstborn child. Now, that's a label that I will own all day long.

✒ Slow Go

Our financial advisor introduced us to the methodology of *"Go Go"* vs. *"Slow Go"* as it pertains to living within your means today in order to maintain your preferred lifestyle in your later years. The general premise is simple: when the cash flow is solid, you should keep your bills paid, support your long-term investments, and enjoy some of life's pleasures with the remaining monies. That would be the mode of *Go Go*.

As you would expect, *Slow Go* is the gear that you shift to when frugality is needed. The focus is on the basics instead of the bright and shiny objects and experiences that we desire. It's about the *needs*, not the *wants*. As my husband can attest, I have a difficult time embracing a frame of mind that is Slow Go. I guess that I just am not naturally wired that way. I can always find a way to rationalize a spend; whether it's a new pair of shoes or a spur-of-the-minute weekend getaway. Needless to say, credit cards are not my friend. However, when it comes to taking care of the kids' needs, my husband and I have never slacked in that area. Those needs were always taken care of first and foremost. Even as all our children are adults with lives of their own, we make sure that they know that we are always there for them. That bottomline is something that we both can agree on!

> *"But when we had an unexpected financial interruption, causing our financial position to slip, it was time for us to push a reset button."*

We've been blessed with relatively stable incomes throughout our marriage. But when we had an unexpected financial interruption, causing our financial position to slip, it was time for us to push a reset button. Looking back, it was a much-needed *wake-up call* in more ways than one.

- **More Turkey Sandwiches**—It's amazing how far a package of deli turkey can go. What I used to pay for one to-go salad for lunch covers a couple of weeks' worth of sandwiches at home.

- **Limited White Tablecloths**—The old adage *Why go out for hamburger when you can have steak at home?* certainly applies to us in more ways than one. You know what? I would compare my husband's cooking to any chef in town, so I don't miss dining out that much. But when we do go out, we are very conscious to keep it in the budget and paid-off each month.

- **More Staycation Time**—We have found a lot of value in spending time at home, sometimes just the two of us, sometimes with family and friends.

- **Less Stress**—Sure, we are working hard at debt reduction and continue to help out our kids while simply living life as it comes. But there is something energizing about that approach. As a result, we find ourselves far less stressed-out in the long run.

- **More Closet Space**—My expenditures on clothes have been cut in half. I have not missed it at all. I did not need all that stuff that would be outdated in six months anyway.

- **Less Automobiles**—It's true: we've discovered that it's possible to live with only one car between the two of us. We've been doing just that for more than a year now! (I encourage you to give that a try if you are empty nesters, or frankly, at any stage of life!)

- **More Joy**—It's amazing how much more appreciation that I have for the little things in life given our "new normal."

"It's amazing how much more appreciation that I have for the little things in life given our "new normal."

So, would I go back to the old ways of Go Go if that opportunity presented itself? I don't believe so. The *mores* outweigh the *lesses*, for sure. I am starting to embrace this culled-down, back-to-basics lifestyle. Though in some ways it was forced upon us, I've long since ripped off the rearview mirror. I'm only looking forward to what's ahead . . . and going slowly while I'm at it.

Are You Truly Busy, Or Are You Going Ghost?

I didn't realize until recently that the term *ghost* (in verb form) dates back to the 1800s. In fact, the earliest use of the verb *ghost* is defined as "to move silently like a ghost." With the role that today's technology plays in our daily communications, it's no surprise that people are taking the easy way out and choosing to be "invisible" in difficult situations. After all, isn't abruptly folding so much easier than facing the ugly hand that's been dealt? Yep, I've *been ghosted*. And unfortunately, I am also guilty of *being the ghost*.

> **"***A partner decides to vanish without notice or explanation. No calls. No social media connection. End of conversation. Period. You have been officially ghosted.***"**

Most often, ghosting is applied to love relationships. A partner decides to vanish without notice or explanation. No calls. No social media connection. End of conversation. Period. You have been officially ghosted. What's even more troubling is that this act of disappearance has evolved into relationships beyond loving couples. Friendships are affected. Business relationships are affected. We're choosing to take the easy way out of uncomfortable situations instead of addressing them head-on.

The problem that I have with this behavior is that we use a myriad of excuses to rationalize playing *Capture the Ghost*. Examples: *I didn't get to your resume. I didn't put you on my calendar. I haven't had time to look over your proposal. I don't have your number in my contacts.* These are all seemingly acceptable responses to inquiries about your whereabouts or lack of responses. But they are way too convenient.

We need to buck up and face the realities of these situations. The job applicant isn't a good fit. So, tell her. She deserves to know. The opportunity that originally existed for the outside contractor simply isn't there now. So, be honest and respond to the proposal. If you don't have someone's contact number, that's on you. Make the effort and find a way to locate it. Quit making that an excuse for *going ghost*.

"When you've been ghosted, it's sometimes easier to just go ghost yourself."

On the flip side, *being ghosted* is hurtful, no matter the situation. As the *ghostee*, you start questioning yourself: Did I say the right thing? Did I do something to offend the person? How much is too much before you throw in the towel and just give up? When you've been ghosted, it's sometimes easier to just go ghost yourself, to live by the excuse that "we are all busy." But that's a crutch, people! We should never find ourselves so busy that we can't be compassionate enough to at least respond. Whether that response is positive or negative—some type of response is much better than no response at all.

Getting ghosted sucks, no matter the circumstance. At the same time though, it's kind of like ripping off a Band-Aid. It hurts really badly for a minute, but it allows the air in to heal the wound that you probably shouldn't have gotten in the first place. Keep working on yourself, and tell the ghosts to get lost.

Stay the Course – Conversation Starters

What are the things that throw your life off-track, and how do you deal with them?

How did your family dynamics play into how your life has progressed?

Do you consider yourself a nurturer? Do you find yourself going overboard in that area, compromising your strength of self?

How has your spiritual journey evolved?

How are you adapting to the physical and mindset changes that are naturally occurring during the multiple transitions in life?

How good are you at balancing the "have-to-haves" and "nice-to-haves" in life?

Is it better to be ghosted or be the ghost?

REFLECTIONS

SECTION 2
LIVE & LEARN AS YOU GO

There is a lot to be said for the mantra *learn by doing* when it comes to just living your life, things like personal and professional relationships, parenting, extended and blended families, adapting to new cultures, and environments. We weren't born with the internal wiring of the HOW TO tackle those experiences the right way every time. That's because there is no textbook on life. You have to live and learn as you go. My mother says that you just have to *"go with the flow."* It's taken me awhile to get to the point where I can get comfortable with the fact that I can't control everything around me. However, I can accept the journey and take in some life lessons along the way.

SELECTED STORIES:

Dig In

Trust in God and Trust in Your Gut

I'm Not Your Friend

Command Performances

Worry About the Things that You Can Do Something About

The Power of the Handshake

Role Reversal: When Your Kids Set You Straight

Friend Breakups

🖋 Dig In

"Two small words: dig in. The phrase may be short, but it carries a powerful punch."

Two small words: *dig in.* The phrase may be short, but it carries a powerful punch. It can be taken as a directive. Or a rallying cry. Or even a motivating statement.

"Sometimes you just have to delve in and seize the moment. I have failed at doing that more times than I like to think about."

Lately, I've been trying to dig into new challenges and opportunities with both feet, rather than tiptoeing around them, contemplating the outcomes. I can't count how many times I have talked myself out of pursuing something different before I even gave it a shot. By the time I mustered up the courage and confidence to go after it, the opportunity was lost. The world moves at lightning speed. That interesting job post on Indeed.com. Upcoming auditions for a musical group. Volunteering to tutor for a semester. Here today, gone tomorrow. It took me four years to pull up my big-girl pants and start writing this book. Not sure what exactly was holding me back. But this experience has taught me a valuable life lesson. Sometimes there's no better time than the present. Sometimes you just have to delve in and seize the moment. I have failed at doing that more times than I like to think about.

Relationships take a lot of digging in. There are layers upon layers of emotions, sensitivities, baggage, and aspirations in all forms of relationships. Strong relationships take work to get past the topsoil and nurture what's underneath the outward-facing exterior. That holds true for all types of relationships involving friends, family . . . and even our faith. If I take time to dig in and focus on what drives me closer to God (rather than focusing on the distractions in life pulling me away from that core), I typically see things more clearly and life gets a lot simpler. But it takes discipline and strength to take on that mindset. And sometimes once I've done the work to dig deep, I don't necessarily like what I discover. Those discoveries require more focus to work on those issues I own. Whew! It can be exhausting. But what could be more important? For me, the answer is nothing.

Dig in was also spoken in my household in the context of diving into a great meal. That same connotation carries into the context of life in general. Life can be mouthwatering. It can be too spicy at times and under-seasoned in others. Life presents unexpected flavors mixed with the tried and true favorites. Growing up, I really wasn't fond of trying new foods or new adventures, for that matter.

I'm making an effort to venture out of my comfort zone and resist the urge to just go with what I know.

It's exciting to think of what I might discover. I certainly have a lot of ground to cover.

Trust in God and Trust in Your Gut

I started my early adulthood on a fairly steady path. I graduated high school and went to college. I spent four years obtaining my undergraduate degree. I got married at twenty-one to my college sweetheart. Unfortunately, the marriage fell apart. After feeling like a complete failure following the divorce, I lived by myself for the first time in my life. That kind of experience teaches you a thing or two about independence, responsibility, and resilience.

"I was really searching for what life had in store for me."

I found myself in Louisville, Kentucky, with no real social or professional networks and no family in town. I felt an urge to get out of town and go start over somewhere new. The best advice that I got during this transitional time was: *Don't make another major life decision for a year's time.* Actually, my gut was telling me that too. So, I kept my job, attempted to go back to school for my MBA, joined some professional organizations, and created new friendships. I was extremely vulnerable and without a lot of self-confidence or self-worth. I threw myself into my faith. I attended religious services, sometimes once a day. Somehow, attending services at random churches with strangers allowed me to dig deeper into my inner self and just trust God to guide me. I was really searching for what life had in store for me.

Then what I *wasn't* searching for happened. I fell in love. His name was Larry. A man fourteen years my senior. A father of four children. A senior partner at the marketing firm we both worked. On paper, it was absolutely the wrong person, the wrong time and place, the wrong life choice. Now after thirty years, I realize that I was in love with Larry almost since first meeting him. But I didn't have the guts to admit it at the time. Enter what I think was a God moment.

Larry was extremely close to his maternal grandmother. When she passed away, I delivered a sympathy card to him expressing how relatable his situation was with my grandmother, Henrietta (Retta), my namesake. It triggered a friendship. Fast forward a couple of years and, even though we were growing closer, we had lots of doubt about entering into a serious, committed relationship. There was the age difference, the mutual place of employment, the financial impact. And a big one—he wasn't sure that he wanted to have more children. Could I accept not ever having children of my own? After all, I adored his kids. What I came to realize is that I adored Larry. He was my everything, and knew that I wanted to spend the rest of my life with him—no matter what. Enter what I think were a few more God moments.

> **"***I think we both surrendered to our hearts (and our guts)
> that we were meant to be life partners, no matter what.***"**

Eventually, I came to the realization that I simply loved him enough to move the relationship forward. For the most part, our families, friends, and work colleagues were very supportive. However, it was not an easy row to hoe. We would break up. Get back together. Make up. Fight. Make up. Until finally, I think we both surrendered to our hearts (and our guts) that we were meant to be life partners, no matter what.

We were married in December 1990 at the church we still call home today. Both families opened their arms to us (although we know that, naturally, there were initial reservations—but those are all far-gone today). Our careers continued to move forward successfully. We have three beautiful children together. I have embraced Larry's four kids with my heart and soul, and they have allowed me to be a big part of their lives. We have eighteen grandkids—and counting!

I often look back and think what our lives would be like if we had not taken the chance. We know good and well that some of our skeptical friends thought that our marriage would never last, much less thrive for more than three decades. That's OK. While we realize that they were just looking out for our best interests, Larry and I know that our love can conquer all.

We are so thankful that God has blessed our lives together. Today, I find that my trust in God is stronger than ever before. I believe that spiritual force is watching over me to remind me to trust my gut, as well.

I'm Not Your Friend

"Come on, Dad; please let me go to Arran's party. It's going to be so much fun, and I'll be responsible."

It was a verbal dance that I often had with my parents during my teens. The conversation went something like this every time:

"Everybody is going to be there, Dad."

"Really, who exactly is **everybody**?" (One of my father's signature responses.)

Reflecting on those typical teenager confrontations, my parents were NOT overprotective. What they were doing is PARENTING.

They truly trusted me to do the right thing and act responsibly (even though my friends were not always angels). My parents considered their primary role to be keeping my siblings and me safe and out of positions that limited our control. They emphasized the importance of having a moral compass, having a sense of self-awareness, and treating others with respect. While giving us freedom to express ourselves, they also insisted on adhering to the household rules. In today's world, I think they would probably be labeled "strict."

It's my opinion that good, old-fashioned parenting, where *"NO means NO"* and *"Because I said so"* applies, is becoming the exception instead of the norm.

After having kids of my own, I have grown to appreciate my parents putting so much of their time and energy in checking the right boxes, while making sure that I understood why they were doing it. But parenting is hard work. Sometimes, it wears me out, even now that our kids are all grown up. I have officially transitioned to adult parenting, which can be equally as challenging as when they were little. But, wow, how rewarding. I still lean on my parents for advice and counsel.

> *"Admittedly, I discovered (especially during my kids' teenage years) that it's not about being popular parents with loose boundaries and no consequences."*

Admittedly, I discovered (especially during my kids' teenage years) that it's not about being popular parents with loose boundaries and no consequences. Good parenting is about instilling strong values, encouraging transparency, building confidence, and supporting your children in all that they pursue in life.

> *"Over time, I come to the realization that being a parent and stepparent is the most important thing I will do with my life."*

Over time, I come to the realization that being a parent and stepparent is the most important thing I will do with my life. Hands down. It can be a thankless "job" at times but as my grandmother would say, you reap what you sow. I am certainly blessed with our harvest. So, back to my terrible teen years . . .

Those tough conversations with Dad often ended with him saying:

"I am NOT your friend; I am your father. You'll understand that one day, Henrietta."

And I certainly do.

 ## Command Performances

Our family is rooted in family traditions—especially during the holidays. My mom and aunts refer to those family gatherings as *Command Performances.*

Dealing with family during the holidays can be the best and worst of times. Politics, religion, sports preferences, and even attire choices can get in the way of a seemingly simple family get-together.

Couple those dynamics with the screaming baby, the cousin that didn't get the Christmas gift he wanted, or the fact that, most likely, 80 percent of the family members have MULTIPLE Command Performances they must attend in a twenty-four-hour period and, of course, this escalates the opportunity for fallouts. It is literally the perfect-storm scenario. And those storms can escalate to hurricanes pretty darn quickly.

Bottom line, holidays come with unrealistic expectations: Calm, homey environments, impeccable decorations, food spreads that could be in a magazine, well-behaved kids straight out of a Norman Rockwell painting. Are you kidding me?

> *"Somehow, those (somewhat-humorous) mishaps turn into legendary stories that are handed down to generations."*

A realistic typical holiday wouldn't be complete without some sort of food-oriented disaster. The bad oysters. The rock-hard Christmas cookies. The vegetables that none of the kids would touch with a ten-foot pole.

Somehow, those (somewhat-humorous) mishaps turn into legendary stories that are handed down to generations, who in turn add to them with their own fumbles.

Honestly, I always looked forward to our family gatherings when I was young. I still look forward to them. Now, I realize that those family times were an important formative and memorable part of my childhood. Today, as adults, my cousins and I *reminisce* about this Christmas or that Thanksgiving. Almost always, we have a big belly laugh that goes along with the story.

> *"It's a fact that all families serve up dysfunction in some shape or manner. So . . . don't fight it."*

Admittedly, I've created my own set of Command Performances for my kids and grandkids. Guess it's in my DNA. However, over the years, I've made a conscious effort to approach these opportunities with a new mindset. Things are not going to go perfectly. I don't sweat the details. It's a fact that all families serve up dysfunction in some shape or manner. So . . . don't fight it.

Yes, I have caught sweet potato casserole on fire.

Yes, I have exploded glass containers on the countertop (luckily no injuries occurred but it meant ordering KFC that year).

Yes, I have gotten in knockdown drag outs with my closest relatives during the holiday gatherings. But blood is thicker than water.

We all have some form of Command Performances in our lives. Throughout the years, I have crafted a formula for getting through them successfully: Take deep breaths. Bow out of heated conversations. Focus on the positives. Go with the flow. And as my friend Terrie would say:

Try not to show your ass!

> *"We all have some form of Command Performances in our lives."*

Worry About the Things that You Can Do Something About

I am a born worrier. It's agonizing at times. At the end of the day, what does the worrying get me? Absolutely nothing. I think that the worrying is driven by my fear of disappointing others, fear of something bad happening to my loved ones, fear of failure, fear of not doing the right thing. So, simply put:

Worry equals fear.

"Worry can manifest itself within all aspects of our lives."

Worry can manifest itself within all aspects of our lives. We worry about how our job performance is being perceived or how people think we are doing in your role of spouse, parent, offspring, sibling, or friend. We worry about our children making wise day-to-day decisions that could have huge impacts on their lives. We worry about our physical appearance, our personality flaws, acceptance from others, or lack of understanding others. Of course, concern over societal and other world problems like environmental issues, international peace concerns, or the political climate has an effect on all of us in the general population. That said, it seems everyone is carrying around that bag of worry.

"I know that some of my personal worries revolve around my current state. Am I where God wants me to be? Where God NEEDS me to be?"

Like most things in life, the overwhelming sense of uncomfortableness that comes over us like a wet blanket emerges from within. Because we might not have all of the answers, because we can't control what's happening around us, we tend to wallow in self-pity and stay up at night. I know that some of my personal worries revolve around <u>my current state</u>. Am I where God wants me to be? Where God NEEDS me to be? I have been very conscious about opening up to those signals, however subtle they may be, so that they may guide me in a certain direction. Rather than being concerned with the total life plan, I'm trying to focus on the one-day-at-a-time cadence. Because it's my belief that God has a unique plan for all of us and we just need to come to grips with the fact that we are along for the ride, no matter the path and pace. In a sense, I am surrendering myself to God. (OK, that's a bit frightening yet empowering at the same time.)

> **"***Get some swagger in our steps, take the reins of what life has handed us, and take the ride.***"**

That said, what about turning this "worry dynamic" on its head? Maybe the best way to combat it is to quit worrying about *who we aren't* and start celebrating *who we are*. Get some swagger in our steps, take the reins of what life has handed us, and take the ride. We all have strengths, so let's focus on those. Let's celebrate what's going well at the moment and encourage others to do the same. After all, the glass-half-full school of thought can be contagious! If you can evoke positive change by taking action, by all means do it. No sense in sitting around concerned about what might happen if things don't go exactly right. My late mother-in-law would often give me these words of wisdom when she knew things were weighing heavy on me:

"Worry about the things that you can do something about."

This is the mantra that I repeat in my mind when I feel a worrying spell coming on. I urge others to do the same.

The Power of the Handshake

My father doesn't know a stranger. It is one of his many gifts. The first time that he meets someone, he seems to effortlessly make them feel as though he has known them his entire life. Knowing the importance of first impressions, he was big on making sure his kids were comfortable with first-time introductions. He worked to instill the importance of being confident and making sure that first "Hello, nice to meet you" was authentic and true to our individual personalities.

> *"One of the first things that I learned about meeting and greeting someone was the significance of the firm handshake."*

One of the first things that I learned about meeting and greeting someone was the significance of the firm handshake and looking the person straight in the eye. No sweaty palms. No limp hand embraces.

Now, take under consideration these learning moments took place circa 1976. I remember thinking how cool it would be to be able to walk into a business office and meet with executives. I think that learning how adults interact made us feel grown up in a way. I always wanted to be older than I was at a given point. "Fourteen going on forty," as my mom would say. (Good gracious, how that mindset has changed!)

How did we master the handshake? Role playing and practicing in our living room played a big part.

"Hello, I'm Henrietta Pepper. So nice to meet you," I pronounced as my twelve-year-old, awkward body extended a handshake to my nine-year-old brother. He would then reciprocate. We would even go so far as to enter through our home's front door to create the sense of a realistic experience. We loved practicing with my Dad too, especially the handshake part. I remember trying to lock in a monster grip and not letting go until he did!

I always get comments about my firm handshake. In my early adult years, I would sometimes be a little embarrassed. After all, I didn't want to come across as too masculine or hard-core. As I matured, I started owning it and embracing the comments as part of my personal brand. Everyone has their own attributes. Occasionally, when someone comments on my confident gesture with "You've got a strong handshake," one will add the phrase "for a woman." I've chosen to take those lobs as backhanded compliments rather than insulting remarks. More times than not, sincere comments about my first impressions are meant to be flattering, and it works to bolster my confidence . . . every time.

> *"This time of social distancing, elbow pumps, and general lack of physical touching demonstrates how it's only human nature to put out your hand for a shake when greeting someone."*

As I write this, it's spring of 2020. The world is dealing with the COVID-19 virus. This time of social distancing, elbow pumps, and general lack of physical touching demonstrates how it's only human nature to put out your hand for a shake when greeting someone. I hope that when this crisis period fades (and it will), we don't make the fist bump our first mode of introduction. And my handshakes often evolve into hugs when I get to know someone well. (Yes, I'm one of those huggers.)

My guess is that we're going to be clamoring for festive gatherings, face-to-face conversations that aren't six feet apart, and actually meeting new people in-person rather than on Zoom or GoToMeeting.com gatherings. At the moment, I'm truly missing the good, old-fashioned handshake and looking someone in the eye. I look forward to resuming day-to-day human interaction. You can be sure, every time I hear a compliment about my death grip of a handgrip, I will continue to give my dad the credit he deserves. Thanks again, Dad.

Role Reversal: When Your Kids Set You Straight

"It's a big reality check when your children call you out on your behavior and they're actually 100-percent correct."

It's a big reality check when your children call you out on your behavior and they're actually 100-percent correct. As a mother, I've spent over half my life attempting to be the best parent and role model for my kids. When mothering my babies through childhood, I focused on the basics: making sure that they had a safe home environment, food on the table, and plenty of sleep. I encouraged them to grow their talents and embrace their passions. My husband and I stood *hand in hand* on the upbringing of our kids. We worked hard to instill strong values and ethics. In terms of education, the mantra was to do the best you can while *giving it your all* in terms of effort. We let them know that they were going to fail at times, but we would never let them become failures. We would be their dedicated supporters all through the twists and turns of their lifetimes.

Once our children became adults, I had an awakening. I came to the realization that, while I had been so busy trying to put on the stoic "mom face" of everyday life, my kids had been absolutely on to me. I had struggled with the guilt that comes with working outside of the home. I didn't love the fact that I missed out on some little moments of their childhood, and I'm sure that resentment shined through on occasion. Our marriage had rough patches, which we tried to keep from the kids. But, as we all know, kids are very insightful, and mine saw right through our "everything is fine" personas throughout that time.

All that said, my children were (and still are) my biggest cheerleaders in life. They loved the fact that I started my own business. They thought that our careers in advertising and marketing were "cool." We got to enjoy a lot of perks with our jobs, which often involved travel transcending into family-vacation time. I could count on my kids to take my side of the argument during extended family disagreements. They would brag about us to their friends, especially as they got older.

Don't get me wrong, the teenage years were not all that great. My girls basically despised me for three years straight, and I never did anything right until they returned home from their first year in college. My son wasn't quite as temperamental, but we had our moments. They have all grown to be caring, loving, talented adults who are thriving in life.

> *"If I had it to do over, I think that I would have opened up more to my kids about how it was OK to be frustrated with life's challenges."*

If I had it to do over, I think that I would have opened up more to my kids about how it was OK to be frustrated with life's challenges. Sometimes I just needed a big cry. Just like it was OK for them to fail, I was going to experience some fails in my life, and it was safe to share those without feeling less of a mom. It was OK for my husband and I to have an argument in order to settle things straight. That's real life in action. I think that I didn't share those difficult moments because I was going by my instinctive nature as a mother *to protect*. But was I really protecting them?

This transparency thing can go off the rails too. Now that my husband and I are empty nesters, things have perhaps gotten a *little too transparent* in front of the kids. A dig here. A jab there. No filters. Our mutual love has never been stronger, but maybe we need to get our parenting game faces (and personas) back on for prime time. Perhaps we've gotten a bit too comfortable letting our raw emotions and irritations come through.

During a recent visit with one of my daughters, she made a comment that stuck with me:

"You know what Mom? Dad and you have not said one nice word to each other since I have been here." And she was right. Our type A personalities were getting the best of us.

"It's just as easy to give a compliment as it is to express a complaint."

Since my husband and I spend so much time together, just the two of us, we've gotten lax about our day-to-day dialogue. Apparently, too lax. We need to get our act together. Especially in front of our kids (and now grandkids). It's absolutely not a good example for them to follow. It's just as easy to give a compliment as it is to express a complaint. I am often the culprit and vow to keep it in check.

So, thank you kids for setting your parents straight. Keep it coming!

Friend Breakups

If you have ever experienced a friend breakup, you know they can be heart-wrenching. In some ways, breaking up a platonic relationship can be more painful than a romantic dissolve. After all, if you split with your partner, you at least have your bestie to lean on. Having been through a couple myself and watching breakups occur within my friends' networks; I keep scratching my head over one question: *Why do we often let the situation get to the point of a "breakup" before we take action to correct whatever the core of the problem is in the first place?*

There are the usual suspects when it comes to friendship troubles. Typically, conflicts arise over a mere misunderstanding around something he said over dinner, or she was overheard making derogatory remarks at happy hour. Friends are notorious for "taking things the wrong way," yet often don't share their feelings into the conversation for fear of "ruffling feathers." So, friends rationalize saying nothing or doing nothing to address their concerns or hurt feelings. What does that solve? Absolutely nothing. In fact, it is the catalyst for the implosion of the relationship as you knew it.

"It's a lot easier to put space between you and your friend than have the adult conversation explaining why you think the relationship is going south."

Aside from the "he said" and "she said" exchanges, jealousy and trust often factor into friendships unraveling. Someone saw your partner with your friend in public (without you). Your BFF got invited to the party and you haven't seen an invite yet. Why do we jump to conclusions before simply addressing our friends with the straight-up question and expect to get an honest answer that would resolve any misperceptions? I have a theory. It's a lot easier to put space between you and your friend than have the adult conversation explaining why you think the relationship is going south. By having an actual discussion, we have to own our part of the unhealthiness, however large or small. But we all know that, in any form of a relationship, it takes two to tango. Both parties must assume responsibility for maintaining open dialogue, acknowledging misunderstood behaviors, and most importantly, nurturing the bond that brought you together in the first place.

I had a friend, Valerie, tell me her BFF breakup (and ultimately make-up) story that really put things in perspective for me. In short, she had been feeling that she was being taken advantage of financially. But instead of expressing those feelings, Valerie chose to bottle them up. While her friend, Joy, claimed that money was tight, Valerie continued to pick up the meal checks and purchase the entertainment experiences—at a moment's notice. Finally, it got to be too much. She blew up. The friendship blew up. Only after a few months of much needed soul-searching did they mend the relationship. Looking back, she says that all that drama could have been avoided if she had only broached the subject head-on when it first occurred.

"Avoiding the "comfort-ation" is just pouring salt on the wound."

This illustration is case-in-point for early intervention when a friendship starts to get uncomfortable. Avoiding the "comfort-ation" is just pouring salt on the wound. That wound may never heal if it neglected for too long.

Hearing that story reminded me of the importance of giving a little more TLC to the good friends I care about in my life. Friendships take effort. Friendships need nurturing. I'm going to work on being a better *friend*. But if I do find myself in an "unfriending" situation, I hope that I can learn from the experience and be a better *person* because of it. We're all works in progress.

Live & Learn as You Go — Conversation Starters

Are you a person who jumps into a challenge with both feet? Or do you just "put a toe in" to test the water? How does that temperament guide your decision-making process?

What keeps you up at night, and how can you positively address those concerns?

How did family traditions help shape your life? How have you established your own traditions?

How can you be more confident in trusting your gut?

Why do we let outsiders influence our decision-making?

At what point are we too comfortable and complacent in our love relationships? What can we do about it?

Are we really investing in our friendships?

REFLECTIONS

Sometimes you just have to sit back and
let other family members have conflict
without taking sides or controlling it (trying)
whether or not the conflict exists
Stay in your lane
Don't be scared of it, just let it
happen, let them learn, and love
them
Sometimes you have to let them fix it, not me

It can be difficult to tell a loved one what you
need, or don't like, much less a friend, its
even harder, but if we did, there would
be less guessing, less hurt feelings,
less resentment on both sides, honesty
would put facts where they are, and
even if it meant being less close
for a while, a true friendship
would pick back up in the future.

SECTION 3
BE PRESENT

As I near my sixties, I have had a huge revelation about the importance of *being present* in the moment. One of my mentors has expressed to me on numerous occasions how he would be disappointed in a person's lack of self-awareness in business meetings, making the point that awareness is expected. He is so right. If the person had taken time to be self-aware of his/her presence, the discussion could have taken a different turn or resulted in a better outcome. The same helpful awareness should take effect when having those somewhat awkward but needed discussions with loved ones. It's so telling when you reflect on how you presented yourself in either a business or personal setting: your body language, your verbal cues (or lack thereof), your attention span. This concept has been a wake-up call for me as of late. I know that I'm not alone when I say that I think there is real benefit in *simply showing up and being present in life*—whether that's in a conference room, sitting on your patio, or enjoying a meal with a loved one.

SELECTED STORIES:

Be Present

Are We Really "Fine"?

Behind the Chair

Rough Patches

Just Breathe

Do Actions Speak Louder Than Words?

 Be Present

> *"It's the new normal to be able to push out work emails, while participating in a webinar, while texting our family members, and downloading documents to print . . . while we're at it."*

Life gets busy. We get busy with life. We are constantly multi-tasking. Technology has armed us with the devices and tools to communicate verbally, with a keyboard, or touch of a finger. And most of us have mastered the ability to do all three simultaneously! It's the new normal to be able to push out work emails, while participating in a webinar, while texting our family members, and downloading documents to print . . . while we're at it.

I believe that the ugly side of technology really shows up in meetings, and not just work-related meetings but also friends-and-family gatherings. Business meetings as we knew them have become obsolete. Back in the day, agendas were issued. People came with reports in hand. Robust discussions were had. Decisions were made. Participants left with marching orders.

Today's business meetings really aren't meetings. Often they are just "check-ins" that are conducted remotely. Is everyone doing what they are supposed to be doing based on the automated project management system? Multiple email strands outline action steps. If you need more facts or information, you need to Google that (or otherwise research it on the internet). No need to waste time conversing or debating. Rarely are there one-on-one discussions happening—even when colleagues are sitting next to each other. And, if an actual physical meeting does occur, the attendees are working on their tablets, answering emails, or stepping out to get that call they had to take because of the text they just got.

> *"When's the last time you were sitting around with the family, having casual conversation without at least half of them being on their mobile devices?"*

This same scenario can be played out at home. When's the last time you were sitting around with the family, having casual conversation without at least half of them being on their mobile devices? I am as guilty as the next person about becoming distracted by my phone while having a purposeful conversation with my husband. The addiction we have with staying plugged-in transcends to friends get-togethers, dinners out with the kids, and even worship services.

Certainly, there are pros around the accessibility and speed of communication advanced technology provides. But at what cost? Have we lost our ability to be truly present? *Present at home. Present at work. Present with friends. Present with our spirituality?*

On a recent international trip, we entered a tiny pub with a prominent sign behind the bar that read:

"There will be no mobile phones or computers in this space. No exceptions. Talk to someone."

Guess this is what it's come to. We actually need to be prompted or even instructed to have verbal exchanges. God forbid that means reaching out and introducing yourself to a stranger and carrying on a casual conversation.

This may sound like a cynical narrative on today's society, but it is meant to be a reminder for self-reflection. Putting it down on paper has caused me to pause and vow to: *be present, more often.*

Hopefully, I won't need a wall sign to remind me!

Are We Really "Fine"?

"Fine." Why are we programmed to spit out that response when asked the simple question, "How are you?" I think that we respond with that nebulous word because it satisfies the politeness factor and enables the conversation to either move on or stop in its tracks.

Fine acts as a shield to keep others out of our personal space. It's the banner that we fly to keep our emotional persona intact and put on a brave face to the world around us. I've made an effort to be more direct with people when they're inquiring about my state-of-being. You know what? It has been refreshing (and in a strange way, cleansing, for my relationships), both professionally and personally.

After all, if you're not being honest about where your head and heart are at the moment, are you coming into the conversation as genuinely as possible? Of course not. But humans are wary of letting people take a peek behind the curtain. We are vulnerable souls. The repercussions of someone actually knowing about your pain, worries, problems, insecurities, or just bad-day moments, are daunting.

I have a work colleague who begins every email with "How are you?" I often wonder what the response would be if I replied, "I am having a really crappy day." Definitely, that's a wet blanket on a conversation starter—or is it? He actually might find it refreshing to realize my current frame of mind so that we may better tackle the challenge at hand.

I think this "Fine" Factor is one that we can all get real around. Dig out of the comfortable shallow ground, and put yourself out there into vulnerable space. Frame your inquiries around real-life context, expressing genuine concern about others' well being. For example, one of my friends is going through a divorce. Instead of asking her how she is doing, I recently approached the conversation with: *"I know you are going through a tough time. How are you coping with everything?"* It really opened up the door into a safe space where she could unload her feelings without hesitation.

> *"Try not to make* Fine *your robotic response to the* How are you *inquiry."*

You have to put yourself on the other side of the conversation too. Try not to make *Fine* your robotic response to the *How are you* inquiry. No, you don't want to vomit out all of the woes of your life, but sometimes putting yourself out there with an honest reply puts the conversation in perspective. It lets the person know what headspace you are in.

"Being transparent is scary."

But let's face it. Being transparent is scary. Being open and honest is letting your guard down. I'm taking more chances and betting on the positive outcomes that will evolve from my newfound approach. And seriously, I'm more than *fine* with that on many levels.

 # Behind the Chair

"We confess our wrongdoings, complain about work, gripe about our spouses, or question a friend's intentions."

Why is it we feel very comfortable telling our hair stylists just about anything? Suddenly, when you plop down in the chair and the cape goes on, it's almost as though the person behind the chair becomes our therapist for the day. It's all about the listening. No "judgey" speak. We confess our wrongdoings, complain about work, gripe about our spouses, or question a friend's intentions. We open up about our kids and key decisions that we're making. All amongst the fake-news magazines that we never get to read at home, good tunes in the background, and the sense of pampering in the air.

"The essential oils used on your scalp are a magic potion that allows you to pour out your soul!"

I was telling my colorist, Jackie, about my book. Admittedly, she says that she's heard it all over the years. She submitted this theory: The hair salon is one of the few places where you are actually being physically touched by other humans. There is that connectivity that puts you in a comfortable, safe environment where you can lean into your emotions. The essential oils used on your scalp are a magic potion that allows you to pour out your soul!

While I concur with Jackie's theory, I believe that it's all about the *listening* part of the stylist-client relationship is the reason this phenomena is so real. Enjoying a personal service combined with a somewhat captive audience (especially a kind or friendly one) makes for honest conversation flow.

> "*You are insulated from the "real world" in that salon space for one or two hours, and it is absolute heaven.*"

The thing about confiding in our stylists is they most often will smile, nod, and earnestly listen to just about anything their clients have to say. With sincere concern. Without judgement. Where else can you actually tell the craziest stories about the *Dysfunction with a Capital D* going on in your blended family? Maybe you've been sucked into the latest neighborhood fiasco. Whatever the situation, you're not going to get pushback or questioned about what your involvement could have or should have been. It's refreshing. You are insulated from the "real world" in that salon space for one or two hours, and it is absolute heaven. You walk out of your session not only feeling better about yourself physically (newly colored, plucked, waxed and trimmed) but you've also taken a load off of your mind. Watch out, world!

I am fortunate to have worked with the same individual stylists for a few years now. Good Lord, they have had their work cut out for them postmenopause! Things have definitely shifted, grown, shed, and taken a life of their own over time 😊. I am so happy to call these individuals my friends outside of the salon. It is still an awesome feeling when I see that color appointment pop up on my calendar reminders, because I know that I get to take a trip to Jackie "behind the chair," and I know that it will be pure bliss!

⚑ Rough Patches

"If you have someone telling you that their union has no flaws—they're lying."

No love relationship is perfect. If you have someone telling you that their union has no flaws—they're lying. My husband and I have been married for thirty years (at the time of publishing this book). We sign off cards, letters, and emails with *My love, forever.* But if I had to sum up our marriage in one word it would be *fierce*. Webster Dictionary defines *fierce* as "showing a heartfelt and powerful intensity of a feeling, emotion, or action." Our picture belongs in Webster alongside that definition!

We are both type A personalities. However, we demonstrate it in different ways. I am an extrovert—taking after my Dad—never knowing a stranger. Adversely, sometimes I can be too loud and outspoken. It takes a lot to make me mad; but when I hit the wall—watch out. My husband, Larry, is more reserved and soft-spoken at his core, with a keen sense of humor and amazing judge of character. Did I mention his quick temper? That's the type A thing.

"We're just now figuring out this whole work-life balance gig."

We immediately connected on our shared love for faith, family, and friendships. We also both have a strong work ethic (which has proved to be beneficial in the grand scheme of things). We have enjoyed success in our careers, but man, we have worked really hard our entire lives. We're just now figuring out this whole work-life balance gig.

We have debates around spirituality and our religious beliefs. We discuss the boundaries and loyalty of friendships. We know both sides of our family are amazing but, like every other family, we have dysfunctionality that we embrace and own. We have our good days and bad.

All said, I can tell you that we have rarely had a disagreement about the raising of our kids. We have been totally on the same page in terms of rules, expectations, consequences, discipline, values—you name it. We've been very fortunate that our separate upbringings (though different in many ways) somehow were grounded in similar roots.

So where and why the *rough patches* in our thirty-year journey together? I boil it down to four categories of reasons:

1) Making Ends Meet

2) Communication Dancing

3) Claiming Space

4) Controlling Control

Making Ends Meet

"However, the grinding financial stress can be overwhelming, especially in those early years of child rearing and later years of education expenses."

Together, we have a total of <u>seven</u> children. As most families experience, there is only so much money coming in and required amounts of money going out every month. My husband and I headed up a typical middle-class family. We stayed gainfully employed. Saved for vacations. Put retirement plans in place. Made sure our kids would be taken care of should something happen to us during their childhood years. However, the grinding financial stress can be overwhelming, especially in those early years of child rearing and later years of education expenses. Seriously, there are times where we didn't really know if we could pay the mortgage, keep the kids in college, and make the car payments.

But that's life and we've coped with it. During the last few years, we have made efforts to downsize our lifestyle, and it's helped ease that stress, but making ends meet is still a main contributor to the rough patches.

Communication Dancing

Communication is at the root of most everything in life. Ironically, my husband and I have both spent our entire careers in the areas of branding, marketing, and advertising. Obviously, these are all disciplines of COMMUNICATION. Even though putting food on the table has been possible because of our abilities as skilled communicators, we find roadblocks in our marriage in this area.

"After a couple of cups of joe, I become a human being.*"*

Let's break this down. It starts in the morning. I literally have a coffee mug with the message: *"Not a Morning Person."* For years, my husband (and entire family and workplace) has put up with my grumpiness and utter lack of communication starting the day. After a couple of cups of joe, I become a *human being.* I'm a poster image for the astrology calendar month of August. So, as fellow Leo's can relate to, once I have come out of my morning daze, I am ready to conquer the world! In comparison, my husband is a late May Gemini—so let's just get that out there. (Geminis are beutiful souls, but you never know what you're going to get each day). Sometimes, he will wake up on what I term "the wrong side of the bed." Early in our marriage, I used to try to "fix" the occasional bad mood he would exhibit. About ten years ago, I realized that we all wake up with a certain optimism or skepticism and that I need to simply accept his.

In terms of ongoing communications, I play the role of keeping communication lines open. My husband would be content just letting things ride—not that he doesn't love me or care about what's on my mind— he's just content with the daily status quo. His attitude is, if there is *really something wrong,* he will hear about it. I tend to attack the issue head-on. If my husband is cranky or seems down in the dumps I start with the questions. "Why will you not open up about what is really bugging you today? What made you wake up on the wrong side of the bed?" You can imagine the heated dialogue (or lack thereof) that is sparked by going down that path.

> *"I'm the needier one. I want him to ask about my day. Listen to my gripes. Tell me that I'm pretty, and yes, tell me if my butt looks fat."*

I'm the needier one. I want him to ask about my day. Listen to my gripes. Tell me that I'm pretty, and yes, tell me if my butt looks fat. I'm a talker and need to get things off my chest. It's important to me for him to listen (or at least pretend to)! I need that level of engagement. Guess I want the more proactive communication instead of reactive communication. You know what? Given the way that we are wired, coupled with our strong personalities, this *perfection in communication* is *not gonna happen*. We have accepted that fact.

> *"In effect, we have created a communication dance that works for us."*

However, we're coming to a better balance of communication these days, probably largely due to our empty-nester status. In effect, we have created a *communication* dance that works for us.

It's very tough when you have little kids running around, when you're wearing a million hats every day, when you're dealing with family, work, and much more. Those were tough years in the communication department of our marriage—but not because we weren't trying. We literally did not have the time to have lengthy, in-depth conversations. If we did find that we had some time, we frankly would have rather slept! It was an exhausting time in our lives . . . that I wouldn't trade for the world! Speaking of winding down, let's talk about Personal Space.

Claiming Space

Space is a big issue for both of us. We both need our individual space. This need usually occurs in the evenings following long, jam-packed days. For me, it's stepping away from it all in my quiet zone—no TV, no iPhone, just space alone; preferably outdoors. Other times, I mindlessly binge watch reality TV shows for hours. My husband has no time for that type of unrealistic reality—and he's probably justified in his disdain—but for me, it allows a disconnection from real life by going to a life so far from my own that it lets my brain wander and actually rest. On the other hand, my soulmate often enjoys his personal space WITH his phone, with the TV on, and probably on social media. That's how he likes to decompress. Other times, he wants to connect with his kids, one-to-one, with some dad time. He really enjoys giving back with his talents, so I will find him ramping-up his creative juices, sketching out new ideas for non-profit organizations. We definitely have learned to find respect for each other's personal space and balance it out. For example, sometimes I want to throw his phone and tablet in the trash and disconnect the TV. Then again, how could I watch my reality shows?

> *"On the subject of space, it's important that we carve out space for just the two of us"*

On the subject of space, it's important that we carve out space for *just the two of us.* When we had younger children in the household, we were religious about Date Nights. Every week, we had one night a week where we got a babysitter and did something together. A movie. Dinner out. A concert. Some simple shared times as a couple to remind us of how much we cared for each other.

We still have date nights.

Controlling Control

> *"Probably, the most predominant contributor for our rough patches is control. Neither of us likes to feel or be controlled. Of course, thinking about it, who does?"*

Probably, the most predominant contributor for our rough patches is control. Neither of us likes to feel or be controlled. Of course, thinking about it, who does? In our case, if either of us gets the feeling that the other is trying to *control* how we spend our time, what we're focused on at work, our family interactions, etc., it sparks heated moments.

When it gets down to how you are driving on the highway or which TV is too loud—isn't that a bit over the top? Unfortunately, we've been there. Couldn't tell you why we both have an inherent need for control. But we both know it's there, and we're accepting of it.

We have grown our relationship over the last few years. We've become closer spiritually. We're stronger in terms of valuing our love and commitment to each other. We have recognized our challenges and addressed them head-on. (Because, you know, we both want to *control* the situation!)

One Day at a Time

We're not getting any younger. Realistically, we're in the last chapter of our marriage; so, we're going all in. Our love for each other remains fierce. We've figured out where the rough patches exist and how to avoid them. If we find ourselves in those places; we are going to hold hands and get through it. The challenge will be which one of us will *control* the pathway forward! I think that I'll just take it one day at a time with my love, forever.

Just Breathe

Somewhere along the way, I forgot to take time to *just breathe.*

I recently attended a women's retreat conducted through our church. Part of the morning session was literally spending a few minutes to breathe with no distractions, no mobile devices, or blaring background noise. I experienced the same type of "mental cleansing" activities at a writing retreat a few weeks later. Those two experiences had an impact on me. So much so that I intentionally carve out a few minutes each day to clear my head and focus on deep breaths. It is miraculous how refreshing it can be.

" The attacks usually hit me like a brick wall with no warning."

I suffer from anxiety attacks. That monster crept into my life when I was in my forties. The attacks usually hit me like a brick wall with no warning. It can be a wonderful day with limited stress and here comes a full-on attack. Over the years, I have accepted that this is an issue for me that I needed to address. I saw doctors and tried different methods of overcoming the anxiety. Interestingly, since I started these "reset breathing minutes," I haven't had near the amount of issues with this condition as I had in the past.

For some reason, I had a lot of shame about my anxiety. I guess that I thought it showed a sign of weakness, especially in the workplace. But I really own it now, and that feels fantastic. This is one area where I can say that getting older is actually a good thing. With age comes a bit more inner peace, more of a celebration of who you are instead of concern about who you are not. I've never been one to stress the little stuff, but now I absolutely don't let petty things drag me down.

"I'm getting better at shoving off that nonsense and focusing on the positive energy that I can bring to this life."

One of my favorite sayings is: *I'm done.* When I've had enough negativity from an individual, or when I have heard an earful of angry rhetoric with no meaning or simply dealing with irrational human beings, I will just say to myself, "I'm done." I then vow to move on to a more positive space. I'm getting better at shoving off that nonsense and focusing on the positive energy that I can bring to this life. I recognize that life is not always going to be unicorns and rainbows. But it kind of is *when I just breathe.*

Do Actions Speak Louder Than Words?

We've all had those awkward confrontations with a friend, co-worker, partner, or spouse. Those situations often end with a series of verbal promises. Promises like, "he is disciplining himself to be more present in the relationship," "she is working harder to be more transparent," or "she is committing to being accessible more often." Flash forward to a week later, and you are back to ground zero. Nothing's really changed. Actions have gone by the wayside. I think that we've somewhat programmed ourselves to overlook those inconsistencies and rationalize the missteps in our relationships and interactions with others.

> *"Oftentimes, people are quite skilled in* talking the talk, *but not as much in* walking the walk, *so to speak."*

The old adage is true: *actions speak louder than words*. However, it also ladders-up to another adage: *easier said than done*. Oftentimes, people are quite skilled in *talking the talk*, but not as much in *walking the walk*, so to speak. So, when I witness people in my life intentionally linking the purpose and meaning behind their words to the way they conduct themselves moving forward, I tend to trust and respect them even more.

Could it be words which have the loudest voice when compared to the actions that happen (or do not happen) in response?

> *"Harsh or hurtful remarks are not easily forgotten and rarely dismissed despite even the most well intended, apologetic gestures."*

It's my belief that words, verbalized or otherwise, can carry a sting lasting well beyond any attempts to make good on those the speaker may regret. Harsh or hurtful remarks are not easily forgotten and rarely dismissed despite even the most well intended, apologetic gestures. There aren't enough dinners out, cards, flowers, or gifts that can readily mend what happens in a relationship when hurtful, impulsive words are spoken. They can piece your heart like a dagger. Conversely, and even more importantly, comforting, loving, and caring words will resonate deeply when delivered with intention and authenticity.

How do we face this dilemma? Will more <u>words</u> remedy a bad situation? Or, will actions or tangible gestures make a greater impact? I'm not talking about text messages or emails. I'm talking face-to-face conversations that get real—real fast. Why is it so hard to say: "I was wrong," "I am truly sorry," "I screwed up," or "I commit to trying harder"? The same question holds true with verbally expressing any unpleasant feelings such as, "I am not comfortable with this relationship," or "I don't feel you are respecting our friendship."

In-person candid exchanges are tough: *Why are you avoiding me? Are you being honest with me? Can we discuss why you've been distant lately? I am not feeling respected as a business partner.* Those types of phrases or questions don't roll off our tongue easily. Maybe it's because if we actually say it out loud, it becomes truth. *Truth* may reveal itself as admitting wrongdoing, acknowledging a weakness, or even admitting a lack of self-worth.

> *"Lately, I'm all-in when it comes to making verbal conversation my first mode of communication. Ideally, appropriate actions will follow."*

No doubt about it, words are powerful. Written words can be compelling and convincing. Yet, spoken words trigger in-the-moment emotions like nothing else can. Tears, hugs, and smiles are reflexes of these powerful interactions. Resolution, a sense of relief, and peace of mind may come as a result. Disappointment, anger, and resentment may dissipate. Lately, I'm all-in when it comes to making verbal conversation my first mode of communication. Ideally, appropriate actions will follow. If not, at least I will have said my piece . . . *from my lips to God's ears.*

Be Present – Conversation Starters

How can we be more comfortable in our own skin?

age, acceptance, self love

How can we honor ourselves as well as loved ones in our relationships?

How can we take time for ourselves and truly commit to that time?

What is our "love language"?

Do we sometimes jump to apologizing in the midst of a conflict, or do we allow time for considering the situation and an appropriate, rational response?

REFLECTIONS

in a negative or stressful situation, you can stay there, worrying, or you can look at the positives and find your way out or through it

SECTION 4
SOAK IT ALL IN

The current methodology around educational-based study is based around *experiential learning*. In literal terms, this is a process of exposing ourselves to real-life experiences. How do our senses relate? Emotions react? Behaviors evolve? With this approach, you are living in that moment and learning from it in real time. Exposing ourselves to new experiences (out of our comfort zone) can be both scary and fulfilling. This is where mindset plays a key role. I am trying to soak it all in and learn from the good, bad, and ugly aspects of everyday life. For a while, I think that I had blinders on, because I didn't want to accept that things may not go my way or the possibility that negatives could potentially outweigh the positives.

I've come to recognize that some of what I perceived as insignificant experiences have in fact shaped my life and who I am today. That is true for ALL of us. As a result, I have been able to create or repurpose those experiences to share with family and friends. Going forward, I'm intentionally promising myself that I'll let life sink in while I marinate in everything it has to offer.

SELECTED STORIES:

Nice to Meet You, Mr. Chrome

Mother Becoming Mom

Self-Diagnosed Imposter

Let's Go Camping!

Suppertime

Be Bored and . . . Procrastinate!

Nice to Meet You, Mr. Chrome

The Thoroughbred industry is recognized for its whimsical (yet intentional) naming of its horses. Often, a new foal's name is derived from a combination of names, taking into account the naming conventions of the horse's lineage. For example, the famous 1930's racehorse War Admiral was the son of the amazing stallion Man o' War, the American Horse of the Year in 1920. Spectacular Bid was the offspring of Spectacular (dam/mother) and Bold Bidder (sire/father). Horses tend to have distinct markings, features, or colorations that are incorporated into their names as well. Sometimes the country or region where the foal resides and/or is trained comes into play.

> **"***California Chrome "the people's horse.***"**

Introducing California Chrome. This stallion was foaled in 2011 in Coalinga, California, USA. As an American Thoroughbred racehorse, he ultimately became the all-time leading North American horse in earnings won. This accomplished horse finished his career as the richest Kentucky Derby winner in history and achieved two-time Horse of the Year notoriety. His flashy white markings, described as "chrome," became part of his name. In turn, it spawned a group of worldwide dedicated fans (referred to as "Chromies") deeming California Chrome "the people's horse."

Enter destiny. A group of industry investors were considering a new business venture and asked me (as a consultant) to attend a preliminary meeting taking place at Taylor Made Farm. It was a gorgeous day in Kentucky. I got to the offices a bit early, and so, was soaking it all in as I viewed the beautiful surroundings and amazing history of the farm. Mr. Duncan Taylor introduced himself and one of his brothers. Like many horse farms in the region, this is a family business that has thrived for generations. There is something magical about the "horse country" region, and the farms that make up its fabric. The specialness goes beyond the impeccable grounds, bluegrass pastures and historical buildings. You can sense the pride in the air. You can feel the daily grit and grind that goes into the upkeep of these farms. So, as scenic as these areas are, it's the people and the stories behind the scenes creating the true essence of the farms' hearts and souls.

> *"Before I knew it, I was looking the horse straight in the eye like we were old friends."*

It was my first time at Taylor Made Farm, and I was asking a million questions as we walked the stone pathways, observing the farm at work in real time. So, I really wasn't paying attention when one of the stable hands strolled out of one of the nearby barns with this magnificent horse. Before I knew it, I was looking the horse straight in the eye like we were old friends. There was not a hint of hesitancy. He had such an easy-going way about his step. We instantly connected.

"Meet California Chrome, Henrietta." I literally gasped!

Of course, I'd seen pictures and broadcast footage of Chrome before; but seeing this creature in his element was a moment I will never forget. The chrome markings were distinct. His chestnut color gleamed in the sun. You could tell he was getting remarkable care and attention and feeling the love. He sincerely made his mark on me.

After profusely thanking everyone for the private introduction, I nervously blurted out:

"My husband is going to kill me because I don't have my phone to take a picture."

Actually, it was one of those moments in time that is better suited as a memory versus a tangible photo. A photo wouldn't have captured the story appropriately.

Thousands of people came from all over the world to visit California Chrome over time. He is definitely a treasure to behold. That farm experience punctuated the importance of taking in the beauty of all God's creations and not taking them for granted. And, oftentimes, it's the unexpected experiences that are the most cherished.

Kentucky horse country is one of the reasons I love the Bluegrass State.

Thank you, Mr. Chrome, for providing that gentle reminder of how fortunate I am to live here.

Mother Becoming Mom

"It struck me that I had the honor of being her mother and the opportunity to become her mom.*"*

Becoming a mother for the first time is a life-changing experience. The journey can be exhilarating, nerve-wracking, exciting, and exhausting all at once. Even though I didn't really know what the hell I was doing, I found this newborn, tiny, little girl fascinating. I found myself just staring at her in awe, bursting with pride, that I had given birth to our daughter, Grace Ann. It struck me that I had *the honor of being her mother and the opportunity to become her mom.*

In 1992, there were no social media support groups or internet to Google the daily questions and concerns every new mother has. So, we relied upon various *What to Expect When You're Expecting* books on store shelves or *Parents* magazines. I was so fortunate to have my mother to provide advice and guidance, yet every day was a new day and every child is different. Side note: I named Grace Ann after my mother. They are still very close today.

The joys of motherhood far outweigh any hard times, but there were *definitely* some struggles. Let's break down the basics.

Sleeping

Grace Ann slept very little. And that's putting it mildly. Therefore, I slept very little. I recall a conversation at the coffee station at work shortly after I returned from maternity leave. I was on my fifth cup of coffee at around 10 a.m. After explaining my zombie-like demeanor from lack of sleep, my colleague replied, "You mean the baby isn't sleeping through the night yet?" I tried to process that before I answered. But I think it went something like, "Well, sometimes she does." That was a complete boldface lie! I was just holding up my shield of new motherhood and protecting my perfect child at the same time. Funny thing is, growing up, my first daughter never slept through the night and still to this day does not require much sleep.

Eating

> "*Then, a miracle solution presented itself unexpectedly: running water!*"

Weighing in at 5 lb., 8 oz. full term, my tiny bundle of joy had a tough time taking in nourishment, yet no problem spitting it back up. For about a year, I walked around with a permanent cloth rag on my shoulder or stain on my shirt! The doctors explained it was colic. So, we managed through it. Then, a miracle solution presented itself unexpectedly: running water! One evening, as my husband tried to rock and comfort her through a colic spell, he leaned over to turn on water in the sink. Suddenly, the crying stopped, her body relaxed, and she was at ease. Hallelujah! From that day forward, the faucet was our best friend.

Mobility

> "*It was during this time that I realized you really have to savor every moment, because before you know it, they are behind the wheel, driving out of the driveway, or walking down the aisle!*"

By chance, we captured our firstborn's first steps on video. So precious. It seemed like only weeks between crawling and walking, though I know it was a longer period. Once she got her walking legs (or "wheels," as we called them), it seemed she never stopped. Well, she really never *walked* anywhere! It seemed she was darting from place to place. She scampered around the house like the energizer bunny. Where did she get that energy?! After all, she still wasn't sleeping much. It was during this time that I realized you really have to savor every moment, because before you know it, they are behind the wheel, driving out of the driveway, or walking down the aisle! It also punctuates how much physical energy it takes to be a parent. As a grandparent, I have such respect for the parents' dedication and relentless effort to raising the kids.

Communicating

From day one, our daughter was very expressive. She started "talking" at a young age. But it was Grace Ann's language. Again, being a new mother, I was unsure of how to handle this development phase. My doctors explained that she knew exactly what she was trying to articulate and to go with the flow and have a conversation with her. Acknowledging that I heard her, she was coming through loud and clear. So, we had many a "chat" session with her in her car seat and high chair, carrying on in her happy voice. Again, I was in awe.

> **"** *Well, I was way too quick to boast about my parenting skills.* **"**

She did love her pacifier ("paci" for short)! Over time, her reliance on the paci became a little *too* frequent. Being a *newbie mom*, I had allowed it to become a habit. She was smart enough to know that too. So, when we began to wean her off the pacifier, she played along. She would demonstratively put it on the table or hand it to me, explaining, "No paci, no paci, Mommy." I admit that I was so proud of the fact that I had taken matters into my hands and broken the "paci habit."

Well, I was way too quick to boast about my parenting skills.

One evening, we were upstairs during bath time. By this time, our second daughter, Christen Ruth, had been born; so, things were getting a bit hectic. (They're only fourteen months apart, by the way.) I quietly opened the door to the bedroom to find Grace Ann standing in a corner, furiously taking a drag off a pacifier. Startled to see me at the door, she quickly ran to me to hand me the culprit. Curious as to where she had found it to begin with, I surveyed the room. Come to find out, she had a secret stash of pacifiers behind her bed liner—probably six or seven. It was hard to be upset with her when she was both adorable in her actions and quite inventive at the same time! Her dad and I still laugh at that story.

Fourteen Months Apart

As mentioned, our second daughter, Christen Ruth, named for my mother-in-law, Ruth, arrived only fourteen months after Grace Ann. It was a planned pregnancy (we got asked that a lot), and we were thrilled. As parents know, no child is like the other, and that rang true for Christen since birth. She was a very calm and quiet baby. She slept soundly almost from the day we brought her home from the hospital. So much so that I found myself jumping up in the middle of the night because I hadn't heard her rustle or whimper. I even confided in my mother, asking, "What is the matter with Christen?" Mom comforted me that she was 100-percent OK and not to be concerned.

That said, Christen did have what we now refer to as HANGRY condition! (That means hungry and angry, for the uninitiated.) As long as her belly was full and her naps were in, she was fine. But if that regime was disrupted, there would be hell to pay! She will tell you that she still has HANGRY tendencies today. Overall, Christen was a sensitive and loving child and still is as a grown woman.

When I was pregnant, we used a baby doll to explain to Grace Ann how to carefully pat her soon-to-be-new baby sibling. "Good baby," she would say. She really took Christen under her wing from day one. They were attached at the hip. People would consistently inquire if the girls were twins. My standard reply was: "No, they are fourteen months apart." Grace Ann will tell you that she remembers that very phrase as one of the first narratives she learned.

Having our babies very close together presented its own unique challenges. Two or double of everything: cribs, high chairs, strollers, changing tables, car seats, etc., etc., etc. You name it. Growing up, they came to wear almost the same size, so there were efficiencies with clothes later on. Like a lot of sisters, they still share clothes to this day!

Baby Boy

In 1996, we were elated when our son, Joseph Cermak (named after his great-grandfather) came into the world. We chose to not learn the gender of any of our kids, so it was a fun surprise when a little boy arrived as the "caboose" of this blended family of seven kids—our "tribe," as we call it!

> "*They say that by the time the last baby arrives, parents are so much more relaxed and less stressed.*"

Born almost two weeks late, Joseph had a full head of dark black hair and weighed nearly nine pounds. Almost three pounds more than my daughters! But he was well worth the wait (and weight!). They say that by the time the last baby arrives, parents are so much more relaxed and less stressed. I am a believer in that statement! After all, you are outnumbered at that point. I remember Joseph being a very chill baby for the most part—good humored with a touch of temper when he didn't get his way. (There is an entire story in the book around the idea of "I'll do it myself" that was inspired by my son.)

Of course, his sisters ruled the nest, so he grew up taking a lot of "orders" from them and following their lead. But you know what they say: boys who grow up with sisters make for great husbands. So, I remind him of that often.

Joseph was athletic, even as a toddler. He loved being part of a team and still enjoys working in teams today. There wasn't a lot of drama in his teen years, so that was fortunate. Especially because we were getting too damn old to go through it! We got to spend four years with only Joseph at home while the girls were away at college. Those were special times that I look back on fondly as Joseph finishes law school.

> "*I think there is a fine line between Mother and Mom.*"

I think there is a fine line between *Mother* and *Mom*. Twenty-seven years ago, I became a *mother*. God provided the gift of motherhood to me multiple times. It's been an amazing journey with lots of seasons and mostly smiles. I readily and happily admit that I am <u>still</u> learning about being a *mom*.

Self-Diagnosed Imposter

Over my years in the business world, I've had my bouts with Imposter Syndrome in the workplace. I've seen my peers deal with symptoms of chronic self-doubt, and I personally have experienced my own struggle to internalize my professional accomplishments. So, what exactly is *Imposter Syndrome?* In short, it is a feeling that you haven't earned success; you simply got lucky and acquired your status "by chance." As a result, people with this condition often retreat internally and resist sharing experiences or ideas for fear of being "found out" and labeled as an *imposter*. Admittedly, I battled this early in my career. Yet as I became a more seasoned professional, I became more confident in my abilities and proud of my accomplishments.

> *"I most definitely have a self-diagnosed case of Imposter Syndrome when it comes to just everyday stuff."*

It's a different story when it comes to my personal life. I most definitely have a self-diagnosed case of Imposter Syndrome when it comes to just everyday stuff. This condition flies in the face of any outward appearance I show others. Typically, I believe most would say I carry myself well with a solid level of self-esteem and resilience. However, my internal battle is always centered on the question: "Am I really doing my best in my personal life (i.e., working on my marriage, contributing to our parish, parenting, nurturing friendships, neighboring, etc.)?" Perhaps the deeper question being asked is, "Have I truly earned all the blessings I've been given?"

I know that I am not alone while experiencing this Imposter Syndrome "headspace." Or should I say *head trash?* Because that's what it really is. And it's only a feeling, not a fact.

> *"Have I truly earned all the blessings I've been given?"*

"Are you fearful you are not measuring-up in the eyes of your partner, friends, or family? Are you simply not feeling worthy of God's gifts and talents, and therefore, are fearful that they will be taken away?"

So, how do we combat it, people? First, I believe you must delve within yourself to discover the root of the problem. Ask yourself some questions. Are you feeling guilty for having to work outside the home, requiring childcare for your kids? Is it brought on because you feel bad that you would rather take a nap than go for a walk with your spouse? Do you feel that you don't measure up to the other people in your life that have similar life circumstances and seem to be dealing with "it" far better than you are? Are you fearful you are not measuring-up in the eyes of your partner, friends, or family? Are you simply not feeling worthy of God's gifts and talents, and therefore, are fearful that they will be taken away?

"But I never would have come to that realization if I hadn't mustered the courage to be transparent with the people I trust most."

I have answered "yes" to every one of those questions at some point in my journey thus far. I have found relief in coming to grips with those feelings. I can own those. But the next step is the important one. You have to share your feelings and experiences with others. For me, sharing is always an eye-opening antidote for my personal Imposter Syndrome. Yes, some of my largest heroes in life are going through the same exact feelings of inadequacy and incompetence that I am. Yes, those feelings have caused them to second-guess life choices that were very purposeful at the time—but don't seem to make good sense now. But I never would have come to that realization if I hadn't mustered the courage to be transparent with the people I trust most. When I finally did, I discovered I also was providing support *to* them, all while I was gaining knowledge and support *from* them.

"When the imposter feelings emerge; you can share some more."

Lastly, we have to be intentional about contributing to that raw dialogue in comfortable, inviting spaces. Places where you start to garner strength and trust in yourself to continue on the best you can. When the imposter feelings emerge; you can share some more. Rinse and repeat. It's therapeutic. It's genuine, healing storytelling at its best.

Let's Go Camping!

Camping out was a frequent activity for my family when I was growing up. We're talking down and dirty camping; not this newfound "glamping" like The Ritz-Carlton outdoors. We would often venture into the woods of state parks, national landmark campgrounds, and sites alongside beautiful lakes and streams with a set of gear fit for the environment. We always traveled as a family unit. Some of the time, it was spur-of-moment weekend trip. Other times, it was a well-orchestrated, multi-day excursion. Regardless of the circumstances, some aspects of camping as I knew it remained the same.

The Ride

> "*Even though we were always encouraged to "look out the windows at the beautiful views," I was perfectly fine lying down in the "wayback," which was what we called the platform. I had my territory marked.*"

Keep in mind, it was the 1970s. So, transportation was inventive in and of itself. Picture the tricked-out family van, complete with a raised shag carpeted platform in the back end for storage and sleeping. I am talking about a state-of-the-art speaker system, built-in shelves, and portable cup holders. Seatbelts were non-existent in those days. Can you imagine that today? Even though we were always encouraged to "look out the windows at the beautiful views," I was perfectly fine lying down in the "wayback," which was what we called the platform. I had my territory marked.

The Equipment

"Despite all that insulation, it still seemed super cold at night. But there was something remarkably refreshing about the fresh air."

Over time, we expanded the size of our tent to accommodate the family sleeping arrangement. But the Coleman stove, knapsacks, coffee pot, big cooler, little cooler, and cooking utensils were staples. Sleeping bags were a must. In colder temperatures, I remember sleeping in my clothes, coat, gloves, and toboggan. Despite all that insulation, it still seemed super cold at night. But there was something remarkably refreshing about the fresh air. In the warmer climates, it would be all about the ventilation—without letting the mosquitoes in. Speaking of which—the mosquito repellent OFF! was a must. We sprayed that stuff on like suntan lotion. It was like the Windex in *My Big Fat Greek Wedding*. That magical liquid cured all things on a camping excursion. Splinter? Spray some OFF! on it. Scrape on the knee? Spray some OFF!, it'll be OK.

We took along our fishing gear on occasion. We all had our own flashlight and knapsack. Can't forget the canteens. These were days before bottled water . . . how refreshing! And I remember crafting a walking stick on each trip where hikes were involved. It was all part of the experience.

"Now, that beat-up-by-a-bear cooler was an excellent show and tell item at school!"

One evening our campsite was ransacked by a bear. Yes, a black bear in the Smoky Mountains! Dad awoke in the early morning hours and just told us to stay quiet. The bear smelled (and obviously located) some jam in the cooler and wasn't stopping until he got to it! We found the cooler down the road the next day with claw marks in the top. Now, that *beat-up-by-a-bear cooler* was an excellent show and tell item at school! Remember when we used to have show-and-tell days at school? Miss those days.

The Look

"It looked something like a cross between someone out of the movie Deliverance *and early Miley Cyrus gone bad.   But what I saw in the mirror was a female version of John Denver and the one and only Olivia Newton John!"*

Early on, I was super into the camping garb. I sported the Levi's and sweatshirts and what we called camping boots. I was a little bit of a tomboy who liked to play tackle football with the neighborhood kids. However, my personal enthusiasm for camping *diminished* as my teenage attitude *grew* ad nauseam. What teen girl wouldn't want to go camping with her parents and little brother and sister versus hanging out with friends on vacation? Right? Somehow, I made my peace with it and basically transformed myself into the fifteen-year-old "cool camper." Picture jean overalls (one strap unhooked, of course), a flannel shirt, a fanny pack, a floppy hat, a bandana, and a guitar in hand. It looked something like a cross between someone out of the movie *Deliverance* and early Miley Cyrus gone bad. But what I saw in the mirror was a female version of John Denver and the one and only Olivia Newton John! Don't you know that I looked ridiculous?

The Location

"We went to outdoor movies in the dark with our flashlights and blankets. No fear. Feelings of freedom. There was so much trust and innocence in the world."

The locations for camping ran the gamut. Tiny campgrounds with no running water to well-mapped camping areas complete with lodges, activities, and programs for the families. We preferred the wooded areas; but that meant a good, half-mile hike to the bathrooms more times than not. That got less and less fun the older that I got!

I don't remember feeling guarded or hesitant to explore new activities in the campground. In fact, my siblings and I would just "go exploring" in the woods for hours on end with the understanding we would be back by dark. We were encouraged to seek out new friends and activities. For example, we learned how to square dance with complete strangers. We went to outdoor movies in the dark with our flashlights and blankets. No fear. Feelings of freedom. There was so much trust and innocence in the world.

We were required to stay on the trail when hiking. My parents were rightly concerned about the pure safety issues of going off the beaten path. I remember wondering what happened to those people who ventured off the grid. I certainly wasn't brave enough to find out. I'm still not that adventurer today.

The Elements

> "*We experienced it all: rain, sleet, snow, and hail. I don't remember it bothering us whatsoever.*"

We experienced it all: rain, sleet, snow, and hail. I don't remember it bothering us whatsoever. We were always dressed in layers. As the temperatures fluctuated, so did our attire. Bear in mind, we would go days without a shower or bath; so, we were probably insulated by grit alone. Again, this was just part of camping out.

It never failed that the weather was not our friend on set up or tear down days. Somehow, the glorious weather on the in-between days and nights made up for the miserable elements. There were always ponchos; so, the hikes, walks, and discovery excursions went on without pause. No umbrellas in sight though. Because that's not *camping*, after all. The only tarp that we had was to keep the firewood dry!

The Meals

> "*We awoke to the welcomed heat of the campfire that Dad would start before we got morning. There was the smell of coffee, hot chocolate, and embers burning throughout the camp area.*"

We awoke to the welcomed heat of the campfire that Dad would start before we got morning. There was the smell of coffee, hot chocolate, and embers burning throughout the camp area. We had three squares a day, no matter where we were. Often, we would dine on the lake or stream for lunch. I remember thinking that canned baked beans, Vienna sausages, and fruit or veggie bags were the bomb. And we got to have *real* Coke or Sprite. That was a treat for sure. Spaghetti for dinner never tasted as good as when eaten around that fire at sundown.

The Souvenirs

I was fascinated by the various state park gift shops. I loved shopping, even at an early age! But there was something about the "minerals" that were mesmerizing. I can't tell you how many boxes of mineral sets were purchased with my allowance. My purchases also included a lot of leather goods, beads, headbands, picture postcards, books, and even Daniel Boone-like, coon-skinned garb. Remember it was the 1970s and I thought it was all cool. Wouldn't it be amazing to still have those items to pass on to my grandkids today?

Camping Out as Parents

The tradition of camping continued with my husband and our kids. Harkening back to our childhood years, we shared the fun and excitement of being outdoors. Camping out during certain school breaks became regular retreats. We enjoyed taking our kids to the locations we used to visit with our families: the state parks, the mountains, the lakes, and the streams.

"*We braved the weather, insisting on campfire breakfasts in thirty-degree weather when there was a Cracker Barrel a mile away! We would continuously repeat: "Isn't this fun, kids?"*

Sure, we had our share of nasty elements, from waking up to ice covered tents to torrential rainstorms when breaking down camp. We braved the weather, insisting on campfire breakfasts in thirty-degree weather when there was a Cracker Barrel a mile away! We would continuously repeat: "Isn't this fun, kids?" Not sure how they would recall those moments! We relished in the challenge of taking the family on a ten-day camping trip with no showers until the last day. Then, what we envisioned as a romantic lodge stay complete with a hot tub would turn into a swim fest with the little ones. Those were joyous days!

There's something about that crisp air, coffee percolating on the stove, and campfire crackling that melts away any of life's troubles and connects you with nature's beauty. It makes me want to go camping again.

Suppertime

My mother is the best cook in the world. I know that is a bold statement, but it is 100 percent accurate. She comes from a long lineage of great cooks. Unfortunately, that cooking gene skipped over me and went straight to my sister, but that's a whole 'nother story! School days started with a hot breakfast, which was not an optional meal according to Mom. Eggs, bacon, biscuits, and cinnamon toast were staples. To this day, I am not a "breakfast person" and have a bad relationship with scrambled eggs; BUT I totally respect Mom's intentions to make sure we started the day out with food in our stomachs.

Lunches usually included homemade soup (occasionally Campbell's Chicken Noodle or Tomato) coupled with a stacked sandwich (always with white bread because that's all we knew back in the day). A lot of pimento cheese, BLT's, and "dressed-up" tuna fish. A pickle and chips on the side.

Every time. Since family lunch meals mostly happened on the weekends, we were always on the go. We would try to get the food down quick and move on to the next thing. Mom would say, "I feel like I'm eating with vultures!"

> *"The main spread of the day was supper. My parents believed in having a "sit-down" dinner every weeknight"*

The main spread of the day was supper. My parents believed in having a "sit-down" dinner every weeknight. No questions asked. It was always a delicious, full-course meal that you could find in *Southern Living*, only better. Mom would spend a good part of the day in the kitchen cooking up deliciousness, which included salad, meat or fish, vegetables, bread, and dessert. No exceptions.

To this day, I've never had better fried chicken, pot roast, pork chops, spaghetti, homemade bread, apple pie, and numerous other culinary delights than what Mom makes.

Wow, I didn't appreciate the hard work and all the creativity that went into that supper making. But Mom never complained . . . *about the cooking part.*

> *"Where it got interesting was the live theater that occurred during suppertime."*

Where it got interesting was the live theater that occurred during suppertime. My brother was notorious for arriving at the table shirtless, and promptly sent back to his room immediately upon sitting down. I would usually show up in a sullen mood, sulking over something ridiculous that happened with a friend or boyfriend that day. There were no phone calls taken during supper. We all had our "assigned" seats around the table. We never wavered from that seating chart, and still honor it today when we gather.

> *"One time I showed up having shaved my eyebrows and penciled them in. And at fourteen years old, I thought that I looked amazing!"*

For some reason, my brother and I found the supper table a stage to take our disdain for each other to a new level. We would mouth *"I hate you"* silently to each other when no one was watching. We would banter back and forth regarding our appearances, the way we chewed, our clothes. I was a clear target, for sure. One time I showed up having shaved my eyebrows and penciled them in. And at fourteen years old, I thought that I looked amazing! I still don't know how my parents kept a straight face. Or what about the sparkling, neon-blue eye shadow that I thought complimented my dark brown eyes? Seriously, what was I thinking? But remember, I thought that I knew everything about everything because I was the oldest sibling. Make no bones about it. By the way, all of this back-and-forth went on with my baby sister quietly eating her meal and enjoying the show.

We had an unspoken "clean-plate rule." Why? Because it was just downright disrespectful if we didn't finish the food on our plates. That's a Southern thing that I love. There were those rare occasions when we would get sent from the table to our bedroom for acting up at the supper table. We learned to watch our step and not take it over the line, because after all, we really didn't want to miss Mom's wonderful dessert!

> **"***My father always raved over the food. It was (and still is) part of my parents' love language.***"**

My father always raved over the food. It was (and still is) part of my parents' love language. Dad will tell you that he can't boil water, so he *literally* relies on Mom for meals. But that works for them. They each have their lanes in the marriage. It has been a successful game plan, as they have been married for over sixty years!

> **"***It truly was a forum where we learned behavior boundaries: when enough is enough and when more is required.***"**

All in all, I look back on those dinners as happy times. We are closer as a family because of them. It truly was a forum where we learned *behavior boundaries:* when enough is enough and when more is required. Somehow our parents were able to take a few moments and talk about their day in a loving, caring manner—despite the distractions. As siblings, we certainly learned to be thick-skinned and, most importantly, to have each other's backs at all times.

Fortunately, on occasion, I still get to enjoy Mom's great cooking around the kitchen table. I take in the conversations and appreciate the opportunity to share the love! I totally appreciate my parents' diligence to make sure that their kids knew the importance of strong family ties and respect for others.

More times than not, those lessons occurred at mealtimes in our household.

I can hear Mom now: "Come to the table, kids, it's suppertime!"

 # Be Bored and . . . Procrastinate!

It's one o'clock on a Thursday afternoon in December. I had carved out time to dedicate myself to writing. Coffee was brewed. Wood burning fire roared in our fireplace with my comfy writing chair perfectly positioned. Mobile phone turned off. Lamp lighting only. I sit down with my computer and journal nearby, for reference. It was the perfect environment for productive writing. So, what happened next? I notice that the rug in front of the fireplace looks really dusty. I get the vacuum out and go to town. Why not go ahead and vacuum the entire first level of the house? Might as well get a load of laundry in, right? While I am waiting on the laundry, I notice my coffee table is full of magazines that need sorting; so, I have at it.

"It is productive procrastination at its finest."

I hate to vacuum. I despise doing laundry. And I absolutely hate anything around organizing things to go in their proper places, whether that's shoes in the closet, pots and pans in the kitchen or paperwork on my desk. But you better believe that I can get real busy with any of those tasks when there is something looming out there that I should tackle right away; however, I just can't get with the program to get it completed. It is *productive procrastination* at its finest.

How many times have I talked myself into taking on the chore of decluttering my office with the rationale it will result in a more efficient, effective work environment. In reality, that's a simple procrastination maneuver preventing me from finishing the work project at hand. I am the master at coming up with all sorts of household tasks when a difficult decision needs to be made or a crucial conversation needs to be initiated. After all, those floors were getting really dusty, and it will give me time to think about what I'm going to say for a couple hours. Then hours lead to days.

> **"***Studies show that managing delay is actually an important tool for human beings.***"**

So, why do we go down the path of procrastination in the first place? Studies show that managing delay is actually an important tool for human beings. Supposedly people are generally happier and even more successful when they are managing delay on their own terms. Maybe it has to do with control.

Life is chaotic and moving at the speed of light. We feel compelled to answer texts immediately, respond to a post within the hour, and God forbid that we let a day pass without responding to emails in our inbox. As a result, we feel an innate need to apply that sense of urgency when it comes to decision-making, conversation-starting, and even apology-giving (when in fact research has proven that delayed apologies are far more effective and meaningful than ones communicated in the moment).

> **"***It turns out boredom actually provokes creativity. If it's the right kind of boredom.***"**

Let's get back to the cleaning as an act of *structured* procrastination. What could be more mundane and boring than cleaning out drawers or vacuuming the house? It turns out boredom actually provokes creativity. If it's the right kind of boredom. For example, sitting on my couch staring at the TV would not fall in that category, right? Wrong. This scenario can ignite new thoughts and ideas. So, when we do make an effort to tackle what we've been putting off, the outcome could be even stronger than it would have been if you hadn't allowed for that headspace reset.

> *"Whether it's dubbed productive procrastination or structured procrastination, it appears to have taken on its own art form in today's society."*

Whether it's dubbed *productive procrastination* or *structured procrastination*, it appears to have taken on its own art form in today's society. Some psychologists are deeming it worthwhile and a positive force. Sounds like I need to procrastinate more often—my house will be cleaner. And I have a newfound appreciation (and excuse) for being bored.

Soak It All In — Conversation Starters

Why don't we take quality time with those close to us?

Why is having a positive mindset so important?

Why do we feel unworthy of having a blessed life?

How can we take in the special moments and possibly set the stage for recurring experiences?

Are we working too hard to try to recreate our favorite childhood memories, or is reliving some memories a good thing?

Why do we beat ourselves up when we are craving some downtime? Why can't we just be OK with that?

REFLECTIONS

SECTION 5
Bring People With You

Some of us consider ourselves born leaders, while others see ourselves as natural followers. Then there are hybrids. Regardless of which category seems to fit you, there is so much value in bringing people with you. For the "leaders" bunch, we sometimes have a tendency to want to "do it ourselves" rather than cultivate a team environment. For the folks who prefer to play a supporting role, it can be intimidating to try to find your own space where you can succeed. This concept applies to business environments as well as family units. Whatever the scenario—whether it is the role of worker, partner, spouse, sibling, or congregation member—we should all find peace by bringing people into our inner circle and being OK with the fails that might occur. Because we know that, at the end of the day, we won't let those individuals become failures.

SELECTED STORIES:

I'll Do It Myself

Coming Home, Y'all

Who Loves You the Most?

The Wisdom of Wine

"There" Is a Moving Target

Room 6

The Shop

I'll Do It Myself

One of the first phrases spoken by my son was, "I'll do it myself." As a toddler, he was fiercely independent and prided himself on being able to accomplish the task at hand without assistance from his sisters or brothers. And he certainly avoided getting help from his dad and me. Whether it was learning how to tie his shoes, ride his bike, or spelling and reading, his attitude was that he could get the job done by putting his head down and not quitting.

I find I have those tendencies, especially when it involves work-related tasks. How many times have I thrown in the towel with the mindset it would just be easier to *do it myself*, rather than taking the time and effort to extend the task to others. By the time that I explained how to go about solving the problem or engaging a group to accomplish the goal, I could have gone at it alone and been done with it with time to spare.

What's wrong with that mode of operation? It's efficient. It produces results. It doesn't suck up time.

While all of those deliverables are positive outcomes, what happens to the spirit of teamwork? You can look at this approach through the lens of the business workplace as well as the lens of family units. As leaders in the business world, we are responsible for instilling a team approach in our work environments. We are better together than when working independently. Or so we've been taught. We've been encouraged to bring people with us: Share goals. Share responsibilities for reaching those goals. Gone are the days of top-down management principles where you are taking orders from the "boss," no questions asked.

Today's world celebrates collaboration. Everyone's voice is to be heard. Everyone's opinion is to be valued. My experience in my family life has seen that the *"let's talk about it"* environment works pretty well on some fronts, but not in others. Though at the end of the day, the buck still stops with the parents to make the decisions. Of course, this can be wildly unpopular, and then collaboration with the kiddos goes out the window!

> *"My experience has proven a collaborative workplace culture to be productive in terms of inclusiveness and creative energy. But what about the tough situations when a yes or no answer has to be handed down?"*

My experience has proven a collaborative workplace culture to be productive in terms of inclusiveness and creative energy. But what about the tough situations when a *yes* or *no* answer has to be handed down? Time is up. End of discussion. I can tell you first-hand that, in those leadership moments, whether it is wearing my CEO hat or my mom hat, it is pretty lonely at the top!

So, I march forward in life in the spirit of inclusiveness and open dialogue. However, sometimes I have to operate in *I'll Do It Myself* mode. That's maybe not as fun or satisfying on some levels, but I can sleep at night knowing the task was accomplished or a decision was made. We awake to another day not knowing what gear we'll need to choose to get things going. That's what makes life so interesting.

 ## Coming Home, Y'all

> *"Reflecting on this time, I thought the "newcomers" into my life were so sophisticated and worldly."*

Junior high school was a change agent in my life. I grew up in what would be termed a "small town" today. I had a best friend (who is still my best friend for life), Karen, and several other childhood girlfriends, all of whom lived nearby. We all went to the same elementary school, participated in Scouts, had sleepovers, rode bikes, and played in treehouses. It was really a time of innocence and bliss.

Then eighth grade came along with the sea of change brought by junior high. Students from all over town were filtered into a centralized city school. Suddenly, my eyes were open to new faces, personalities, and upbringings. I was introduced to students with varied ethnic backgrounds. I experienced different cultures and traditions. Reflecting on this time, I thought the "newcomers" into my life were so sophisticated and worldly. I found myself a little envious of the ease in which some of the girls exhibited bold personalities. They seemed more "city-fied" than me. More expressive and confident. Yet they were very inclusive and inviting. I was intimidated, excited, and enlightened—all at the same time.

> *"Friendships were minted. Lifetime bonds were formed. I don't think that our solid, close-knit group of girlfriends realized the impact that those relationships would have on our lives moving forward."*

Friendships were minted. Lifetime bonds were formed. I don't think that our solid, close-knit group of girlfriends realized the impact that those relationships would have on our lives moving forward. The experiences we shared helped shape us as individuals. I grew up a lot in those two years of junior high.

Life moved on to high school. More new people, experiences, and relationships. There were first loves, breakups, and make ups. Our group of girls made the most of having lots of fun together, but not at the expense of others. Yes, we had our share of mischievous episodes and typical high school drama, but when all was said and done, we came out of those four years pretty darn OK.

Some of the girls went on to college, others explored new passions and talents, or moved to different cities and states. We were all developing into young adults. I think that those post high school years solidified how special and unique those early teenage friendships were. There is something so gritty about understanding your girlfriends' DNA and what makes them tick. You can finish their sentences. You know that something is up by just looking into their eyes or certain tones in their voice.

> *"Sometimes in person, and always in spirit, we were continually there for each other."*

Marriages were celebrated. Children were born. Careers emerged. Families evolved. Life became blended. But the specialness of the close BFF bond we had formed was always valued and came to the surface when one of us was suffering, celebrating joyous occasions, or simply hitting a bump in the road while navigating life. Sometimes in person, and always in spirit, we were continually there for each other.

We're all in our fifties now. While we're all leading different lives, our *common ground* lies in caring for our families, guiding our adult children, and enjoying the rewards of grandparenting. Divorces have happened. Tragedies have been endured. Faiths have been tested. Jobs have been lost. Businesses have been started. Love was lost. Love was found. Financial distress happened. Financial prosperity came. Family struggles occurred. Family joy bloomed. We've come a long way since those junior high years. Yet in terms of our link to one another . . . literally nothing has changed.

> "*Thank goodness it was too cold for bathing suits—you can visualize that picture. We talked like it would be fun to gallivant around in our bikinis, but let's get real. Just sayin', we aren't in junior high anymore, and neither are these bodies that we call our temples!*"

Recently, ten of us middle-aged ladies were able to come together for a reunion of sorts. A modest two-bedroom, one-bathroom cottage on the inland waters of Gulf Shores was transformed into a haven for fireside chats and late night reminiscing about the shenanigans we lived through. Thank goodness it was too cold for bathing suits—you can visualize that picture. We talked like it would be fun to gallivant around in our bikinis, but let's get real. Just sayin', we aren't in junior high anymore, and neither are these bodies that we call our temples!

So . . . it was cozy PJ and sweatpants attire for the duration. We were never hungry, thanks to our fabulous hostess and chef! There were salads and homemade soups. Healthy snacks coupled with chips and beer. Chocolate and wine. Coffee and sunrises. Cocktails and sunsets. Beautiful beaches and calm waves. We even had our own stylist on hand to get us all spruced up for our one night out on the town.

We were lookin' good, or so we all thought. That's all that matters.

There were intimate one-to-one conversations about personal struggles and tough decision-making. We celebrated successes. We cried about losses. And then there were the shared experiences about the harsh and hilarious realities of postmenopausal living. Heck, you might as well laugh about it! It's the new normal for us all.

> *"Though some of us had not physically seen each other in decades, it was as if we had just left our high school graduation in 1981. It was like coming back home."*

Though some of us had not physically seen each other in decades, it was as if we had just left our high school graduation in 1981. It was like coming back home. It became a celebration of our bond and the impact it has had on us all. I think that I kind of took it for granted over the years. Now, I'm committed to embracing and treasuring these remarkable females for a lifetime.

God bless y'all, BFF Girls from BG.

The Wisdom of Wine

> *"These sessions really caught on. The ideation process was fluid, productive, and ultimately successful in generating innovative initiatives."*

Let me state up front: *I love wine.* There is something about the robust taste of a good Malbec or the crispiness of a chilled Chardonnay that relaxes my brain a bit and allows me to open up (no pun intended) to new ideas and conceptual thinking. I had a client, now a good friend, who liked to gather our synergistic group of creative firms to generate ideas after work. The hook? Giving everyone a chance to enjoy a glass of wine (or other beverage) off the clock. These sessions really caught on. The ideation process was fluid, productive, and ultimately successful in generating innovative initiatives. These "every so often" sessions morphed into regular dates on our calendars. The scheduled meeting times became part of our individual monthly regimes. So much so that we gave them a title: *wine-storming sessions.*

So, was it the wine that was the catalyst that made these brainstorming (oops—wine-storming) sessions so productive? Or was it something else that stimulated freethinking and collaboration at its best?

After all, *not all* of the participants were drinking wine. Some weren't drinking alcohol at all, for that matter. So, what was with the "wine factor"?

"Thinking about it, the simple answer is unstructured structure.*"*

Thinking about it, the simple answer is *unstructured structure.* First, the structure part: it was a feat getting us all together in one <u>physical</u> spot. The meeting request wasn't positioned as a call out for a mandatory meeting. Rather, it was a relaxed invitation to get together with our associates and think out loud. No bad ideas. No judgements. Just freethinking. Second, this somewhat-unstructured format infused a little fun factor into the traditional brainstorming arena, which allowed the collective group to focus on the process rather than a goal of leaving a closed-door session with all the answers. Sometimes the creative juices would flow effortlessly. Other times, we would struggle with landing on the "big idea," yet we never left the table feeling like we had failed each other or the idea behind these gatherings. Perhaps the ideas just weren't there that day. Perhaps we just weren't getting the wisdom vibes from our vino.

"We chose a patio venue. The flowers were starting to bloom. Derby time in Kentucky was approaching. There was a sense of anticipation in the air."

I distinctly remember one of our wine-storming sessions in the spring. We chose a patio venue. The flowers were starting to bloom. Derby time in Kentucky was approaching. There was a sense of anticipation in the air. We assembled with very intentional objectives in mind. We needed to engage a client's internal associates with a new branding program that we were introducing for the business. Surely, we could come up with great ideas on the patio, with wine in hand. Well, that didn't happen.

> "*What was intended to be an ideation session around business turned into a session about navigating life as a new season approached.*"

What did happen was bonding. We started to talk about the personal pressures we were feeling as spring was springing. Houses were being put on the market. Preparations for summer activities were underway. Much-needed vacations were envisioned. The realization that the year was almost halfway complete was at hand, and we all were trying to be cautiously optimistic about the outlook and forecast for the future. What was intended to be an ideation session around business turned into a session about navigating life as a new season approached. How refreshing. It helped bond the group by bolstering trust and creating a transparent environment where we could go beyond our work boundaries to build deeper relationships—beyond the definition of "colleague."

So, let's toast to wine-storming. And may we all be the wiser by sharing in the moment.

Who Loves You the Most?

> "*So, though the words* I love you *weren't necessarily spoken with a high level of frequency, they were <u>always</u> felt.*"

Love. It's such a universal emotion, yet everyone has their own love expression. Reflecting on my childhood, though we didn't verbalize our love for each other in an *over-the-top* manner, I *always* felt very loved. I knew that it was unconditional love. Unwavering love. Eternal love. So, though the words *I love you* weren't necessarily spoken with a high level of frequency, they were <u>always</u> felt.

Interestingly, my husband and I have gone to the total opposite extreme with raising our kids and in our roles as grandparents. There is literally not a conversation, email, social media post, or even text that doesn't include an *I love you* somewhere in the mix. So, what's the right balance?

"Does too much "love" in your vernacular somehow dilute it?"

Does too much "love" in your vernacular somehow dilute it? But does repeating the expression time-and-time again make it simply more habitual and seemingly less heartfelt? What is driving you to say those three words? For me, I truly want those I love to know that they are important in my life and that I have them in my heart. Saying it "out loud" makes it real, not just implied.

I've noticed that as I get older, I've extended my *I love you's* to people outside of family. My close friends, who I adore and would find it hard to live without. My church "family," with whom I've shared the most glorious and saddest of times. My choir "family," who celebrates God with words and music melodies throughout the church year. My work-related network of friends, who have shared the thick-and-thin moments of work life.

I guess my new love MO (mode of operation) has come about because I have FINALLY come to realize that it's the people in your life who matter most. Nothing else really comes close. Except God.

What about the God-love? I am leading a remarkably blessed life. I try every day (more than once) to let God know how appreciative I am of the blessings that He has bestowed on me and my family. I make it a point to let Him how much I feel *His* love. My children have taught me how to better express my love of God and creation through their Christian journeys. For that I am eternally grateful.

So, back to our family and friends. How much love expression is too much? I guess that the answer is not universal. For some, it's speaking the words. For others, it might be expressed nonverbally with a hug or a gentle touch on the shoulder. Or maybe a text with a heart emoji.

For me, I say it often and I say it loudly (coupled with the hugs and emojis), especially when it comes to my family members. I try to not let an opportunity pass without letting them know that they are loved.

When my son Joseph was a little boy, we established a verbal exchange that ends every one of our conversations:

"Who loves you the most, Joseph?"

His reply: "Mom."

I know he knows that no one will ever love him like I do.

In fact, that sums up how I feel about all my cherished family and friends.

I don't think I can say *I love you* enough.

"There" Is a Moving Target

Why are we obsessed with getting "there"?

I want to get there by the time I reach fifty years old.
I want to arrive in that place sooner than later.
All I am focused on is getting there.
Reaching that place in life is so important to my career and family.

So, exactly where is *there?*

There might mean a personal, family-centric, faith-based, or professional goal that you're aspiring to conquer. It might be defined as a personal space you hope to occupy in providing equal energy balance for your mind and body. *There* might be the financial threshold that you've been working to achieve your entire life. We all have that head trash of where we "think" we should go and where we truly want to go. What is steering us? Where are our guideposts? How do we keep true to ourselves without sacrificing our loved ones along the journey?

"*So, exactly where is* there?"

Recently, I had a conversation with a friend about anticipating the infamous sixty-year-old milestone and what that might feel like. My immediate response was that it felt pretty great. Let's tally up my assets. Strong faith. Safety and health. Amazing family. Solid friendships. Why the pause? For me, the catalyst was self-inflicted identification as an "overachiever." By my own doing, I strived to have it all: love relationships, family, career, friends, blah, blah, blah. And frankly, I did a pretty good job of getting "there." That life-analysis got me thinking about a new outlook on life.

> *"Why don't we start thinking about the "there" being our satisfaction of our inner selves?"*

Why don't we start thinking about the "there" being our satisfaction of our inner selves? After all, if people were content with *just being,* and less concerned with achieving, wouldn't the achieving part happen organically? Maybe that point of view contradicts my belief in capitalism, which I feel built the United States. But does it? Striving to work harder, be a better friend or soulmate, be a better parent or daughter or sibling are all good goals. Yet, not at the sacrifice of your true, inner self. Otherwise, it's all an act. Upon reflection, I wish that I had set my sights on what I could achieve in terms of personal goals versus the goals that society placed upon me. I wish that I had traveled more at a young age. I wish that I had explored further education earlier in life. I wish that I had adapted a healthier lifestyle sooner than I did. I wish that I hadn't rubbed baby oil on my skin in the broiling sun when I was a teenager! I wish that I hadn't been so mean to my parents in heated moments growing up.

> *"Choose something in your life to fight for."*

When it is all said and done, I have very few regrets in life. While reflection on our pasts is important, we must constantly be looking forward to what's possible. So, here's the challenge that I am taking on myself. Choose something in your life to fight for. Take up a hobby. Read more. Embrace nature. Take some classes to learn something new. Exercise the way you want to—not how society tells you to do it. Get out of your comfort zone and meet new people. Explore new cultures. By doing so, you are going to take others with you. Movements will be formed out of passions. I guess that it's less about reaching ***there***, and more about the journey of ***getting there***.

 # Room 6

My close group of friends in college remains my best friends today. My roommates in the Chi Omega sorority house at the University of Kentucky, a.k.a. Room 6, are connected as kindred spirits.

> *"Housed in a tiny room with two sets of bunk beds, a couple of small closets, and lots of hot rollers and awful '80s fashion attire, we were living the college dream and a few hot messes!"*

Housed in a tiny room with two sets of bunk beds, a couple of small closets, and lots of hot rollers and awful '80s fashion attire, we were living the college dream and a few hot messes! I would be remiss if I didn't mention that my closet was in the hallway, but that's a whole other story. This is way before the computers and cell phones, so things happened in real time on a daily basis. There was full-on transparency and very few secrets between us. We experienced being in love and breakups, schoolwork challenges, ridiculous friend drama, and a few keg parties along the way.

Since leaving college and going our own directions, we have remained close. The conversations have shifted to marriage and extended family, children and grandchildren, home life and work life. Yes, there's still a tiny bit of self-inflicted drama sprinkled about, but that is far from the root of our closeness.

> *"I know what real friendship means and continuously attempt to recreate that magic."*

Through the years together, we learned the importance of being true to ourselves and celebrating who we are as individuals. That authenticity was and is special. Even though we are very different people, we share a lot of the same values. We had each other's backs in those days, and that continues even today. I know what real friendship means and continuously attempt to recreate that magic. But I don't think Room 6 is replicable.

So, a Two Keys cheers to you, Karen, Kym, Nancy, and Sheri. You sincerely helped shape me into the woman that I am today. I love you all.

 # The Shop

My husband's grandfather, Joseph Cermak, arrived in the United States from Czechoslovakia in the early 1900s. At twelve-years-old he spoke no English, and his family basically was starting over in a new country. He fast tracked through elementary school, quickly adapting to the everyday life in Ohio. After marrying his wife, Ann Marie, he settled in Southern Illinois and started a commercial glass company from the ground up. Southern Glass was a successful family business. Its core commercial and residential business served housing communities, office spaces, churches, automotive showrooms, etc. In the latter years of business, it expanded into decorative items such as lamps, wind chimes, frames, and jewelry cases.

> *"Affectionately referred to as* The Shop, *Southern Glass employed family members and folks from outside the family."*

Joseph's only child, Ruth, and her husband, Albert "Al" Profancik, eventually worked into the business and carried it into the next generation. In fact, it remained a family-owned and operated business for more than seventy-five years until its closing in 2019. Affectionately referred to as *The Shop,* Southern Glass employed family members and folks from outside the family. Eventually, all employees united under the family business umbrella, taking pride in the craftsmanship and creativity coming out of the Centralia, Illinois, facility, day in and day out. Ruth, my mother-in-law, literally worked six days a week, every week, until the day that she passed away in 2018 at age eighty-eight.

My husband was not a part of the day-to-day operations, as he chose a different career path after college. So, I'm sure that we weren't privy to the inside embers that would sometimes take fire amongst the family members working in the business. But *I am sure* that there was a unique specialness to that workplace that should be acknowledged and celebrated.

This is a family of coffee drinkers. So, personalized mugs hung on the rack above the coffee pot. Al preferred weak coffee, so everyone just dealt with it, never complaining. Everyone had his or her work area. Looking back, that footprint was ahead of its time. Now offices are going to an open floor plan with unique spaces carved out for individuals to claim as their own.

> **"** *Bells on the front door welcomed customers all day long. You were always greeted by name. If you weren't known when you walked into the shop, you certainly were known by the time that you left.*

Bells on the front door welcomed customers all day long. You were always greeted by name. If you weren't known when you walked into the shop, you certainly were known by the time that you left. The showroom was modest, but it always showcased a new design or technique by one of the family members. There was so much talent exhibited over the years.

> **"** *The showroom was basically telling a story of the family throughout the generations.* **"**

Enclosed in glass, the natural light would hit the displayed items and project amazing streams of color. Of course, the showroom would be sprinkled with pictures of grandchildren, great-grandchildren, graduations, weddings, etc. The showroom was basically telling a story of the family throughout the generations. Holidays were celebrated: Christmas trees, Easter baskets, Halloween décor. There was a playfulness that made you feel like a kid in a candy shop.

"The sense of pride that was multigenerational. That's what is so special about family businesses, no matter how large or small."

As the family began closing the business, stories started to emerge—stories about the early struggles, keeping up the pace when business was booming, navigating the recessions, etc. But mostly, the stories revolved around the people. The skills and talent that the family members each contributed. The integrity that resonated throughout the business and into the community. The sense of pride that was multigenerational. That's what is so special about family businesses, no matter how large or small.

In essence, Southern Glass represented seventy-five years of *hard work,* producing magnificent *works of art.* But to me, it will always be *The Shop.* It felt like home every time that I heard the bells as I entered the front door.

Bring People with You – Conversation Starters

What pressures do we inflict upon ourselves?

Why do we see the need to push ourselves to do "better" instead of enjoying where we are in life?

Are we doing a good job of letting people into our lives? Why are we hesitant to do that?

Are we taking time to treasure and celebrate our relationships?

What are we doing to express our love to those who need to feel it the most?

Do you believe in Best Friends Forever?

Family businesses succeed largely because of a shared work ethic. For those of us in a family business work environment, how do we best navigate the challenges?

REFLECTIONS

SECTION 6
RISE ABOVE IT

*R**ise above it!** My Grandmother Retta expressed this mantra throughout my childhood, and it still lives on in our family's vernacular today. It is actually at the core of my inspiration for writing this book. Not a week goes by that I don't have some connection with those three words. I was brought up with the philosophy of: God first. Family second. All the rest falls into place as it should. You have to work at life. After all, if life was all easy, it wouldn't be as interesting.

They call it "work" for a reason. It ain't easy to hold a job and excel. *Relationships* take work. Working on *yourself* takes work. This section is all about taking the high road, accepting hardships, getting real with our emotions, and doing a reality check on where we stand in this lifetime. Sometimes we need to take a hard look at ourselves in the mirror and *rise above it!*

SELECTED STORIES:

Happy Derby

It Takes A Lot to Scare Me After What I've Been Through

Holiday Cookin'—Southern Style

Shoulda-Woulda-Coulda

The Hot-Mess Express

Why Do We Worry So Much About What Other People Think?

Sometimes You Need a Good Talking-To

Happy Derby

"Even though there were no fireworks, foot races, parades or steamboats ushering in the big day, it still felt special. It was Derby Day 2020."

The weather could not have been more beautiful. The sun was shining. There was zero humidity in the air. You could sense the familiar smells of freshly cut mint and newly poured bourbon, roses and clean cut grass. Even though there were no fireworks, foot races, parades or steamboats ushering in the big day, it still felt special. It was Derby Day 2020.

There were a lot of imperfections to the seemingly perfect day starting with the date. Instead of waking up to the first Saturday in May, we awoke to September 5. The COVID pandemic had taken hold of Derby, just like it has hundreds of events around the world, causing a delay of the running of the Kentucky Derby for the first time since 1945. The glorious Churchill Downs was quiet in the stands due to a ban on spectators—again, thanks to COVID. There was the realism of the social unrest happening in our city as well around the world. Peaceful protestors stood outside the track, eager to have their voices heard.

Despite all of the uneasiness that was surrounding this surreal day, there was still a feeling of anticipation and excitement leading up to that greatest two minutes in sports. We sat glued to our television, watching the remarkable horses prep for the races.

"The vibrant Paddock would be filled with cigars, Oak Lilies, Mint Juleps, guys and gals with beer carts, and pop-up vendors displaying their wares."

Typically, the commentary and cameras would be focused on the sea of colorful headpieces, high heels and cowboy boots, the loud sport coats that would never see the light of day on a normal Saturday afternoon, coupled with the gussied-up visitors dressed to the nines. The vibrant Paddock would be filled with cigars, Oak Lilies, Mint Juleps, guys and gals with beer carts, and pop-up vendors displaying their wares. Private jets would circle overhead. Chants would boom from the infield. Sounds of oohs and ahs would echo from the clubhouse to the grandstand, along with the cheers of victory and cries of defeat. The venue would become increasingly littered with betting tickets and programs as die-hard enthusiasts headed back to the wagering windows for one more attempt to win "the big one."

> *"As the afternoon unfolded, it was as if the pageantry and materialistic facets had been lifted. Indeed, it was the* spirit of humanity *rising to the occasion."*

After all, those are the sights and sounds that make the Kentucky Derby so special. Right? Yes, maybe on the surface. However, 2020 presented an entirely new perspective on the spectacle of spectacles. As the afternoon unfolded, it was as if the pageantry and materialistic facets had been lifted. Indeed, it was the *spirit of humanity* rising to the occasion.

Jockeys proclaimed their gratitude for just being healthy and able to do their jobs. They expressed their desire for human equality in this uncertain time. Breeders, owners, and trainers seemed to rally around each other as though to overtly demonstrate the compassion, heart, and soul that is at the core of the Thoroughbred industry spanning over centuries. All were quick to point out the skill and dedication of the unsung heroes working on the backside of the track. Emotions were high. Tears were shed unapologetically on major news networks. Accolades were verbalized for the otherwise non-visible folks that make the horses safe, cared for, and prepared for their big day. Sentimental stories were shared about family and friends navigating through difficult times.

Those raw displays of emotion were coupled with the celebrated staples of Derby: Steve Buttleman's bugel introducing each race and moving performances of Kentucky's state song. Donna Barton Brothers's real-time interviews with the winning jockeys, capturing the transparency that comes with triumph. Local news anchors recalling the impact of Derby to our community, both on and off the track.

As Authentic sprinted to the finish, I thought it to be ironic how his *name* was reflective of the tone that we had witnessed throughout the day. Somehow the imperfections of the day had brought out some of the best in genuine people. Interestingly, it left me with an overwhelming level of respect and appreciation for the Thoroughbred industry that maybe I had taken for granted.

Clearly, the pomp and circumstance of a typical Derby Festival in May was missing this year. Somehow I still managed to end the day happier than when it started. That's the magic of the Kentucky Derby.

It Takes A lot to Scare Me After What I've Been Through

"Even though the moments in time are long gone and perhaps even resolved, why is their sticking power so strong? It's like they're tattooed in our brains!"

There is a scene from the movie *Sex and the City* where Sarah Jessica Parker's character, Carrie, is roaming through a Halloween costume shop with her friend Amanda after recently being left at the altar by her long-time love, Mr. Big. She is confronted with a screaming five-year old with a scary mask running straight at her. "It's going to take a lot more than that to scare me after what I've been through," she remarks after being run over by the little goblin.

Isn't that the case when we go through the not-so-pleasant seasons of our lives? When you survey your life span, hopefully the good memories outweigh the bad ones. But it's always those bad experiences that seem to take a front seat. You rewind the scenarios in your head over and over. Even though the moments in time are long gone and perhaps even resolved, why is their sticking power so strong? It's like they're tattooed in our brains!

"For the first time in my adult life, I felt super vulnerable and defeated."

To compound the issue, I feel like the more I try to drain those memories from my head, the stronger they dig in. I'm in my own self-inflicted house of negativity, and I can't seem to get out. Well, look in the mirror, sister. You hold the keys. I recently went through a really difficult period of time. My professional life wasn't where I wanted it to be. Communication in my marriage was wobbly. Difficult conversations were occurring on the home front. My financial position was off. For the first time in my adult life, I felt super vulnerable and defeated. Frankly, I was scared to face what was staring me in the face as the new normal for my family, career, and lifestyle.

So, I had to make up my mind to address the situation head-on. Quit pushing rewind and push the reset button. That doesn't mean that I have to forget about those negative situations. However, rather than wallowing in the self-imposed "pity-party safe space" filled with watching *Real Housewives* reruns, I needed to get on with what was next.

"The genesis for this book is about learning from what life throws you and embracing those learning moments in moving forward."

The genesis for this book is about learning from what life throws you and embracing those learning moments in moving forward. So, I'm on that road to recovery now. But it is not an easy path. So, I'm giving myself time: Time to acknowledge what I've been through. Time to recognize my positive behaviors during turbulent times.

My skin has gotten thicker but I think my mind has become more open. My willingness to forgive has been strengthened. The most valuable outcome of this whole season of my life has been my ability to empathize with those people around me who are experiencing hard times that I can't even fathom. Everyone truly has some type of cross to bear and is likely grieving someone or something. It's reaffirmed for me how important it is to begin each day with gratitude for all the blessings I've been bestowed. I'm determined to use these past experiences to help others and now am armed to face the next set of challenging times . . . because they will come.

But now, *it's going to take a lot more to scare me* too, Carrie Bradshaw!

 ## Holiday Cookin'—Southern Style

> *"I will say that holiday cooking is a tradition on both sides of our families. The kitchen apron comes out of hiding, and I really try to focus on bringing my limited culinary skills to life."*

I own the fact that I am not the best of cooks. I can cook pretty well when I put the effort into it, but frankly, it's just not my passion. And my husband is an awesome cook and enjoys it, so why bother, right? I will say that holiday cooking is a tradition on both sides of our families. The kitchen apron comes out of hiding, and I really try to focus on bringing my limited culinary skills to life. Or, in some cases, I let Kroger do the cooking and let my decorative serving pieces do the talking! Just being real, folks.

It was a tradition on my husband's side of the family for my mother-in-law and father-in-law to cook the main entrée (usually turkey) as well as a couple of simple stovetop sides like beans, rice, or pasta. Each of the five siblings' families would be responsible for a side or dessert. My sisters-in-law were (and remain) wonderful cooks. They continue to amaze me with their tasty dishes, some go back generations and others are brand new to the family.

> *"If you are in the South, you know the usual suspects: whipped sweet potatoes (complete with marshmallow topping), jellied cranberry salad, squash casserole, mandarin orange gelatin molds, hot-spiced applesauce."*

Looking back on my early years of marriage, I faced my most challenging times in regard to holiday dish creations. I was raised with the Southern staples of Thanksgiving, Christmas, and New Year's. If you are in the South, you know the usual suspects: whipped sweet potatoes (complete with marshmallow topping), jellied cranberry salad, squash casserole, mandarin orange gelatin molds, hot-spiced applesauce. The list goes on.

I realized early on that, coming from Czech Republic heritage, my husband's family had no clue as to what these Southern-inspired dishes were by the looks and smells of them. Of course, they had their own food traditions at the holidays with regional dishes such as marinated cucumbers, kielbasa, stuffed cabbage, and even liver-ball soup. When they didn't go after our weird, Southern-style dishes on the counter top, it wasn't because they were unappetizing (hopefully), they just preferred choosing what was familiar and comforting to them. Can't say I blame them. So, it was a real dilemma for me each year as to what to bring come holiday time. I wanted to choose something everyone could relate to and would enjoy eating. Of course, I had to be realistic about what I would be capable of preparing—nothing too advanced! It got to be a running joke with my husband and me. And honestly, it became a tad bit stressful.

> *"And then, several years ago, I had an epiphany. Everyone likes chips and dips. Cheese and crackers usually draw a crowd."*

And then, several years ago, I had an epiphany. Everyone likes chips and dips. Cheese and crackers usually draw a crowd. Catch the early arrivals with food—while they're starving and awaiting the main spread. Problem solved. So, I began "being in charge" of the appetizers. Spinach Dip in Hawaiian Bread bowls was a favorite. (Thanks again, Kroger!) Pimento cheese. Bugles and dip (who doesn't like some Bugles?). I've even ventured into beer cheese and celery with cream cheese on occasion. All were welcomed with open arms and eaten up.

> "*Since we all have matured a bit, it has become less about the food and more about the love and care in the room. But we still like to eat well!*"

Although my mother-in-law and father-in-law have since passed away, we still have our traditional holiday gatherings and dish assignments. My sister-in-law hosts the event. It's a blast each year. Since we all have matured a bit, it has become less about the food and more about the love and care in the room. But we still like to eat well! As we prep for this year's Thanksgiving, my husband walked in one afternoon very proud to announce that he had gotten my food assignment. It was something that he thought would be right up my alley: buttered noodles! *Yes, buttered noodles!*

I just hope I can pull it off. Seriously! Either way, I'll probably still make a run to Kroger to pick up some chips and dip, for old time's sake.

Shoulda-Coulda-Woulda

One *thing* that really irritates me *about me* (believe me, there are many), is finding myself reliving life moments that didn't necessarily turn out the way I wanted and asking, "What would I have done differently?" These moments encompass everything from a disagreement with a friend, to a debate with a colleague, to contemplating an important, strategic business decision.

How could I have handled it for a better outcome? What should I have done to find a stronger solution? It's the stuff that keeps you up at night.

> "*The first step on the road to recovery is recognizing the problem. Right?*"

It's the *Shoulda-Coulda-Woulda thing.*

The first step on the road to recovery is recognizing the problem. Right? I know that this is an issue for me, so I've established a bit of a litmus test to validate (or not) my actions of the past AND help guide me when future situations arise:

Did I fully understand the situation at hand?

Did I handle the situation with the utmost integrity?

Was I honest and ethical?

Did I consider all parties involved?

Was I biased by my own personal beliefs?

Was I true to myself?

Did I call out falsehoods when they needed to be called out?

Did I have the facts, or did I make too many assumptions?

Did my emotions get the best of me?

Was I really listening, or was I just digging in my heels?

Was I letting someone take advantage of me?

Did I sincerely give it my best effort to resolve the situation?

"It starts with me. I must keep myself accountable."

I recently went through a client breakup. They were increasingly dissatisfied with the work and dissolved our working agreement. Those breakups are never easy, even in the best of circumstances. Honestly, in that particular situation, some of the boxes in the litmus test were checked . . . and some were not. However, it taught me a valuable lesson: It starts with me. I must keep myself accountable. Talk the talk and walk the walk.

"Most importantly, leave it behind, because not leaving it behind you will suck the life out of you."

My lasting remarks on the subject—definitely, try to stay clear of the *Shoulda-Coulda-Woulda* land once the situation is resolved or dissolved. Most importantly, *leave it behind*, because not leaving it behind you will suck the life out of you. When I'm going through tough situations at home, work, or with friends, Mom will tell me to this day: "Honey, you did the best you can, now move on."

 # The Hot-Mess Express

"As I've gotten older (and wiser), I've tried to distance myself from these types of situations, primarily because, most of the time, these scenarios lead to a hot mess!"

I am guilty of joining in on a juicy conversation around the latest gossip, trending topic, political rhetoric, and "he said/she said" BS. Why is that temptation so hard to resist? It's not substantive. It IS going at the topic in a totally subjective manner. By participating in these types of dialogues, I'm not demonstrating my best behavior, because I'm just glomming on to the conversation at hand. As I've gotten older (and wiser), I've tried to distance myself from these types of situations, primarily because, most of the time, these scenarios lead to a hot mess!

The outcomes are never good. Feelings are hurt. Secrets are revealed. Untruths are perceived as gospel. Why? These types of topics are rarely rooted in the right groundwork for productive debate or consensus building. It's all about personal opinions and less about objective feedback, sharing knowledge, and providing constructive insight.

This type of confrontation happens beyond social environments. It happens in the workplace, within families, and among faith-based communities. People tend to pick sides and close off their eyes and ears to others' points of views because they are so resolute to not "give in."

Social media has given us a new platform to express ourselves. But are we leveraging that in a positive manner, or are we hiding behind it?

It's awfully easy to jump onto a groupthink trail. I see this phenomenon dramatically affecting the young people in my life, in some ways for good, and in others, for worse. Technology is both a treasure and a curse where twenty-first century human interaction is concerned.

> *"Maybe the better action is to simply walk away and revisit it with a calmer mindset in a day or two."*

Aside from social media, these situations also arise in public spaces. Heated discussions turn into verbal (and sometimes physical) confrontations. Again, the temptation is to lean in to make sure that your voice is heard. Maybe the better action is to simply walk away and revisit it with a calmer mindset in a day or two.

Regardless of the communication methods available—from mobile devices to social media platforms to old-fashioned face-to-face conversations—I am being very purposeful in my actions and gauging when it's best <u>not</u> to board the *Hot-Mess Express.*

Why Do We Worry So Much About What Other People Think?

I am a smart, confident woman with positive energy and a good sense of humor. I believe that I'm likeable and generally can engage people fairly easily. I have my own style that I am completely comfortable with and enjoy trying new things with my look. I readily admit my faults and celebrate the talents that God has given me. Simply said, I am comfortable in my own skin.

Why then do I take pause to be concerned about what other people think about how I look, how I conduct my life, or what decisions I make personally or professionally? Realistically, why do I care at all? We all are guilty of saying "I really don't give a #X!# what other people think." But is that sincere?

> *"I don't believe that we are worried about what people think;*
> I believe that we are worried about what they will do."

As humans it's baked into our DNA to want to be liked, accepted, and, even more deeply, loved. Underneath the layers of the outward façade that we show others are innate emotions clamoring for someone to embrace and accept them as who they are. So, if that's the case, why are we not more transparent with the fact that we actually DO care what other people think? My theory is this: I don't believe that we are worried about what people think; *I believe that we are worried about what they will do.*

Case in point. If I am planning to make a business presentation glammed-up in a stylish dress and heels, it's because that's what makes me feel confident and at my best. So, why might I have the tendency to go back to the closet and put on a more casual outfit? Because I am skeptical the audience might not find my first impression relatable; therefore, the account opportunity may be lost. So, it's their *actions* I fear.

If I am contemplating whether to participate in the gossip conversations going on at work, am I really worried about what my work colleagues will think if I choose to walk away? No, I'm worried that they will find a way to exclude me from future dialogue or even shun me from the work group all together.

> *"I sincerely don't give a darn about what people think, but I*
> *sure do care about what actions they might take."*

I have been going through this internal struggle, specifically as I've been writing this book. How many times have I delved into the unproductive space of asking, *"What will people think?* About the content? The writing style? My storytelling? *What will they think about me!?"* And I have come to the realization that I sincerely don't give a darn about what people think, but I sure do care about what actions they might take. Actions like: write a terrible review, blast me out on social media, tell me that I'm not good at this. So, I need to get OK with those possibilities and get on with the job of getting on.

Well, the lesson I'm learning about going through this journey is that you don't need to worry about what people think (or do, for that matter) as long as you are true to yourself and have conviction in what YOU are doing. I am standing tall in that dress and heels and walking away from the gossip-filled conversations. Most importantly, I own this book. I own the person who I am today and the person who I will become as the years go by. And that's what I think about that.

 ## Sometimes, You Need a Good Talking-To

"The behavior-change expectation would be clearly articulated, along with how they were going to help us get there."

My parents believed (and still believe) that the way to get through to us as children was to sit us down and have what we referred to as a "talking-to." These were not conversations. These were straight-up, direct narratives on why you should or should not be acting in a certain manner. The behavior-change expectation would be clearly articulated, along with how they were going to help us get there.

It was such a deliberate way of communicating. It certainly motivated us to take action, because it was crystal clear what the issues were and how we were expected to remedy whatever behavior was awry. It made us *accountable*. I have used the "talking-to" method to discipline my kids and have to say that it's been effective for the most part. However, where I have seen the most successful outcomes has been employing the "talking-to" in work environments and friends.

For whatever reason, I think that people struggle with accountability today, with owning their behaviors and responsibilities to work teams, friendships, love relationships, family members, etc., etc., etc.

Could those struggles stem from a *lack of accountability* to ourselves? It starts from within.

If you want to pursue a passion that you have in life, you should do it and not let anything get in your way. Sounds a lot simpler than it really is, correct? Life gets crazy. Barriers get in the way. Dreams go by the wayside. On the other extreme, if you find yourself in a harmful relationship, you should get out of it. Again, sounds simple. But maybe guilt sets in. Maybe you start blaming yourself. Why don't we stand up and be accountable to ourselves first?

> *"Somehow, my self-esteem suffered. My confidence was wavering. It was basically "do-over" time."*

I recently experienced a career transformation after selling the business I founded fourteen years ago. It was an emotional roller coaster. I thought that I had a master plan that could be flawlessly executed. I could seamlessly flow into my next chapter. Well, life happened. Unexpected bumps in the road. Somehow, my self-esteem suffered. My confidence was wavering. It was basically "do-over" time.

As I conversed with a colleague (and friend) about taking steps towards employment, I was telling her about job opportunities I had seen posted online. I thought that my credentials were up to par. I was feeling pretty good about my chances of at least getting a few interviews. I was rambling on about "what if" this and "what if" that. What I didn't see coming was a "talking-to":

"Listen to yourself, Henrietta. With thirty years of experience, being a successful entrepreneur and business leader, you <u>THINK</u> you might get an interview? You need to contact all of the companies you <u>might</u> be interested in working with and tell them what value you can bring. You are a seasoned professional, and they would be fortunate to have you work for them. Get your big-girl pants on, and get ahold of yourself!"

> *"Get your big-girl pants on, and get ahold of yourself!"*

Translation: <u>I needed to stop being a victim and start being accountable for my actions moving forward.</u>

That was raw language. It was a game changer for me. I suddenly was inspired to get an action plan down on paper. My confidence was boosted. I was motivated to take on some new challenges and pursue new passions (like writing this book). Every now and then, I will give myself a "talking-to," just to make sure I own my behaviors and am being true to myself.

Rise Above It — Conversation Starters

How can we tackle awkward family dynamics with a smile?

Why is it hard to move forward from a negative situation?

Why is sucking it up so difficult?

How can we do a better job of leaning into our support system?

Do we worry too much about what others think about us? What situations cause us to put up our guard?

Do we really want people to be direct with us, or would we rather have things delivered sugarcoated?

REFLECTIONS

SECTION 7
EMBRACE & ENJOY

Today's the first day of the rest of your life. That phrase has stuck with me since I was a kid. Somehow, it is really resonating with me as of late. Maybe it's the season of life that I am living and reaping what I have sowed. Maybe it's the realization of the fact that I'm not getting any younger! No matter the catalyst, I am finding comfort in waking up each day focused on the simple pleasure of finding gratefulness and gratitude. This section focuses on those simple celebratory moments of joy we might be taking for granted. After all, we don't get a *do-over* in this lifetime. Embrace life to its fullest!

SELECTED STORIES:

There's No Place Like Keeneland

Family Night

Realists Or Clapping Monkeys—You Need Both

Lack of Sleep Has Awakened Me

Penny's Palace

Live for Moments of Joy

Dear Retta

Stories Shape Our Reality. Reality Creates Our Stories.

There's No Place Like Keeneland

Nestled in the Bluegrass region, at the center of the Thoroughbred industry, stands Keeneland Race Course in all its glory. Since 1936, the course has captured the hearts of millions. Ironically, many of its visitors may have initially been lured by its best-in-class racing facilities or its world-renowned horse sales lying in *the cradle of the breeding industry*, as they say.

> "*However, what ultimately creates the everlasting love affair with Keeneland for most of us goes way beyond the horses.*"

However, what ultimately creates the everlasting love affair with Keeneland for most of us goes way beyond the horses. It's the unique racecourse experience that you cannot duplicate anywhere in the world. The experience transports you to a place where the simple pleasures are transformed into unforgettable indulgences.

First Impressions

Keeneland was first envisioned by business man and horse enthusiast, Jack Keene; thus its name. The course endured its share of financial hardships and trying times over the years. However, the beautiful limestone-inspired structure and park-like grounds still carry Mr. Keene's original vision of a special place that sweeps you away for a few hours. It's where world-class entertainment meets world-class racing, embracing you with home-like, comfortable surroundings.

> "*I was struck by the entrance surrounded by the overhang of trees sprinkled with the plantings that coincided with the season. I could see the impressive yet inviting limestone facade ahead.*"

Circa 1981, I was a college freshman at the University of Kentucky. It was the first weekend of the Fall Meet and my first visit to Keeneland. My outfit was classic preppy: Madrice blazer, pink IZOD shirt, and khaki skirt with needlepoint belt. I remember thinking that I looked so grown up. I was struck by the entrance surrounded by the overhang of trees sprinkled with the plantings that coincided with the season. I could see the impressive yet inviting limestone facade ahead. However, I was mesmerized by the hundreds of tailgaters that had already set up in their cars' waybacks or trunks. My carload of friends slid into a parking spot. Clearly, Keeneland had me at hello!

Keeneland has been a National Historic Landmark since 1986. No doubt, this designation will allow it to evolve organically without disrupting its historic charm. The former President/CEO of the Breeders' Cup said it well, "[Keeneland is] one of the most storied and celebrated racecourses in the world."

Meet You at the Paddock

" *The tranquility of the clear skies and scenic view transcended into the structured chaos that is part of the racing experience as hoards of people poured into the track.* "

I made my way up the short walk to the entranceway with two friends. The tranquility of the clear skies and scenic view transcended into the structured chaos that is part of the racing experience as hoards of people poured into the track. I made it through the turnstile, purchased my program (and a pen of course) so that I could pretend I knew what I was doing on the wagering side of things. I wanted to look the part. (My bets are still based largely on the name or the horse or colors of the jockey's silks, but that's all part of the fun of it.) Leaving the tailgating area, we were given the all too familiar instructions: Meet you at the Paddock. We headed that direction.

The Paddock at Keeneland is like no other racecourse. It is literally and figuratively the meeting ground for all. It's the first place that you see when you come into the main gates. Vendors and shops line the parmeter. There is something for everyone: logoed t-shirts and hats, fascinators and fedoras, cocktails and candy, bowties and boots.

> *"You can't recreate the feeling that you get when you lean into the Paddock rail with people of all walks of life and all parts of the world."*

Horses enter the Paddock area under the shade of trees that have probably stood strong for decades, maybe centuries. You can't recreate the feeling that you get when you lean into the Paddock rail with people of all walks of life and all parts of the world. Everyone has one thing in common. They are there to experience the one and only Keeneland.

Food that Travels

For most general attendees, a day at Keeneland means a day on foot. That doesn't preclude you from indulging in local bites that will leave you wanting more. That's part of the experience that keeps visitors coming back! From the decadent carved corn beef sandwich to the signature burgoo, the food is just downright delicious. And you can't beat the extra swirls of homemade ice cream cones that delight the kid in all of us.

> *"That chilly day in October, that tasty Burgoo helped warm me up and was easy to carry as we made our way out to the stands."*

Prior to that day, I had never tasted burgoo. Now I am addicted. It reminds me of my mom's homemade beef and vegetable stew with the crunch of a gumbo-like texture. That chilly day in October, that tasty Burgoo helped warm me up and was easy to carry as we made our way out to the stands. After all, we were there to see the races! We were quickly at a standstill among the crowd of young people gathered right at the fringe of the grandstand. Apparently, the entire UK campus had descended upon Keeneland.

And They're Off!

The socialization extends out to the area aside the tracks. Sure, there is plenty of seating available, but on a crisp day in the fall or a sunny, breezing spring day, you are likely to find many spectators arm in arm on the rail, trying to get a bird's eye view of the horses in action. There is nothing like that thunderous boom as the contenders make the last turn and head toward the iconic deep green finish line post.

> "*So, you were left to observe the race in its most purest of forms. As I watched in awe, it felt like I didn't have a care in the world.*"

That day the dirt track was clean and smooth and running fast. The turf track (my personal favorite) was groomed to perfection, glowing with that unmistakable blue sheen that Kentucky is so famous for. We had made our bets. As we waited for the start, we looked behind us to the Corporate Suites and admired the stunning attire of whimsical hats and colorful suits that the "older" visitors were wearing. There was a tad of envy running through my head coupled with a bit of relief that I was in that place in life without a lot of responsibilities (beyond my own well being). I didn't realize until later how short-lived that period was to be. I'm so glad that I embraced it.

Suddenly, the gate opened and the horses were off. In those days, the announcers didn't call the races over the public sound system. So, you were left to observe the race in its most purest of forms. As I watched in awe, it felt like I didn't have a care in the world.

The Living Room of the Bluegrass

> "*It's like entering into a living room filled with people you don't know and, by the end of the day, you are making plans to visit each other again.*"

There are a few unexpected gems tucked within Keeneland's uniquely intimate grounds. A roaring fireplace with comfy chairs welcomes you into the Clubhouse area. With the proper credentials in hand, you are escorted up a hand carved wooden spiral staircase into the myriad of dining areas. Tables have designated seating; so, you could find yourself sitting with a quiet couple who have been visiting Keeneland for forty years, an up-and-coming young business man navigating his way through Kentucky as part of a new career endeavor and an international tourist checking off one of her bucket list items. That's one of the unique aspects of Keeneland. It's like entering into a living room filled with people you don't know and, by the end of the day, you are making plans to visit each other again.

> *"It was about gaining an understanding of the horse farms, the art and science of the training and horse ownership with a focus on the sweat equity that goes into it all."*

My love for Keeneland continues. My husband and I introduced our kids to horse farms and the sport of racing early on. Obviously, it wasn't about the wagering. It was about gaining an understanding of the horse farms, the art and science of the training and horse ownership with a focus on the sweat equity that goes into it all. We continue to celebrate birthdays and other special occasions at Keeneland. We reunite with old friends at the Paddock, take in The Hill for some retro tailgating, attend weddings, and frequent special events. On occasion, we have the opportunity to enjoy entertaining colleagues and friends in a reserved box, an experience that I had aspired to all those years ago.

> *"The course's historical story of grit, strength, and perseverance offers a gentle reminder of what's possible as we enter the dawning of a new day and time in the aftermath of a pandemic."*

Keeneland could not be a more perfect backdrop for the 2020 Breeders' Cup. It's the place that the Breeders' Cup originated. It is consistently ranked one of the top ten tracks in North America. Its beauty is to behold. The course's historical story of grit, strength, and perseverance offers a gentle reminder of what's possible as we enter the dawning of a new day and time in the aftermath of a pandemic.

My Keeneland story began in 1981 as a simple indulgence—a day trip away from the college regime. The story continues with each chapter punctuated with one consistent theme: there's no place like Keeneland.

Family Night

> *"It was sacred family time. The kids looked forward to it and deemed it a* must-attend *event each week that they labeled as "Family Night."*

Some of my fondest memories are from Family Nights. Starting when the kids were about five and under, every Friday evening we would order pizza, spread a tablecloth on the den floor, pull out the bean bag chairs, and plug in a rental movie (or two). In the winters, we would start a wood burning fire in the fireplace. It was sacred family time. The kids looked forward to it and deemed it a *must-attend* event each week that they labeled as "Family Night."

Those evenings were so valued that the children would chastise each other if someone even *considered* spending the night out with friends or going to a game on Fridays. My husband and I were equally as committed. After all, it was not only quality time to enjoy with our children, but it was a chance for us to be together and just chill after a long week of work.

Family Night continued each week until the kids went off to college. Circa 1999, I didn't realize how important those Friday nights were on so many levels. Unconsciously, we were carving out consistent dedicated time for just family. I don't think that is happening enough with today's families. I hope that I'm wrong.

The technology advancements of the internet, social media, mobile devices, etc. are barriers. Why would a fourteen-year-old today want to watch a movie with Mom and Dad in the den when they could watch it in their room on a tablet? Today's parents also are guilty of being glued to their phones and computers way too much. The accessibility and need to stay plugged-in is just too tempting.

> "*Kids' schedules today are jammed packed with sports activities, organizational involvement, school events, and so on. Parents are equally time-starved.*"

Technology aside, I submit that the strongest two catalysts for the scarcity of designated family time are 1) the reality of the hectic cadence of family life and 2) a lack of commitment to make it happen. Kids' schedules today are jammed packed with sports activities, organizational involvement, school events, and so on. Parents are equally time-starved. They become glorified bus drivers. They're on call with work practically twenty-four seven (thanks again to technology). They have business obligations beyond regular business hours. So, the availability of time is definitely a factor in diminishing quality family hours.

> "*On the bright side, it's never too late to start new family time activities that will eventually transcend into traditions.*"

But even if the time is available, I don't think that families are making the commitment to dedicate that time to family togetherness. That's a sad commentary on today's incredibly fast-moving lifestyle, but it's a fact. On the bright side, it's never too late to start new family time activities that will eventually transcend into traditions. The precious memories will abound. It starts with making regularly scheduled family time and holding everyone accountable.

I still look forward to Family Nights. Even though now, as empty nesters, it's typically just my husband and me sitting by the fire with a glass of wine.

♠ Realists Or Clapping Monkeys—You Need Both

OK, I admit it. I am a dreamer, an eternal optimist, and a poster child for "serial entrepreneur."

> *"That said, I am trying to be more conscious about when it's time to get out of the blue sky and get down to the deck."*

That said, I am trying to be more conscious about when it's time to get out of the blue sky and get down to the deck. This recent adaptation to realism has not come easily. I've had some real screwups in both my personal and professional life, so you could say that I learned by doing.

> *"The ultimate reason this endeavor failed was my inability to reach out or up to my peers and family for guidance."*

When you combine a big-picture thinker with a resilient "get 'er done" mindset, the result is not always stellar. I tend to fluctuate between those two schools of thought on a regular basis. There was a point in time when I got real with myself. It was 2005 when I started a branding business on my own. I had a second business start-up fail in 2008. Why? I spent too much time in the clouds, dreaming about what that business could be as opposed to realistically fleshing out a clear, realistic vision and strategic plan. The ultimate reason this endeavor failed was my inability to reach out or up to my peers and family for guidance. Also, I still was in the infancy of my first business start-up and should have been laser-focused on building that foundation. Indeed, my original venture went on to be a successful, profitable firm for fourteen years.

So, the life lesson resulting from that experience was the confirmation that I needed help. Imagine that.

I needed a personal board of advisors—a designated group of trustworthy people to be brutally direct with me while also encouraging me to explore new ideas. In essence, I needed a few realists and a few clapping monkeys on that board.

My husband is a realist by nature, but he also is my biggest cheerleader when I need it. And then there is my banker and financial advisors. Talk about real! These people have my back and will yank me back in line when I go "squirrel." Then I have my clapping monkeys that will get up in the clouds with me and dream, dream, dream. There are endless possibilities. Opportunities abound. There are effectively NO bad ideas when I have these people around me.

The sweet spot is finding a balanced group of trusted folks to keep you in check who also encourage you to think freely. Because some of those dreamy ideas are going to materialize. When that happens, everybody wins!

This concept doesn't just apply to my professional life. When times are tough for me personally, I absolutely need my enthusiastic, glass-half-full supporters to rally around me and try to get me out of my self-induced funk. Let's go have fun and forget about it.

The realists are equally important in those situations, reminding me of what a blessed life I'm living. As the saying goes, at times I just need to slow down and smell the roses and be satisfied with the new normal. Other times, I need a swift kick in the rear to bring me into reality. Enter the *realists* in my life.

I've created tools to help me through this mind game. I started a journal to park all of my ideas—some are genius, some are ridiculous—but all are inspirational for me.

> "*True entrepreneurs are not afraid of trying and failing. In fact, they are afraid of NEVER TRYING. I fall in that category of venturer and discoverer.*"

I highly recommend putting things on paper because it makes it real. After all, ideas are just ideas until you write them down and make them tangible. You may end up executing on some of those ideations. And if you fail, you are absolutely going to learn something from that experience to apply to another quest. For me, I may fail a lot, but failure is not an option. True entrepreneurs are not afraid of trying and failing. In fact, they are afraid of NEVER TRYING. I fall in that category of venturer and discoverer.

I think my dreamer mentality is driven by me wanting to cram as much as I can into this life while I still have time. Certainly, I am not alone in that arena. A business colleague of mine includes "accomplishing world peace" as an integral part of the company's vision/mission statements. Why not, right? I am clearly one of their clapping monkeys! Or wait a minute—I think I might be a realist. Regardless, everyone needs both groups in their lives.

♣ Lack of Sleep Has Awakened Me

We've all had our personal issues and angst around dealing with the impact that the COVID-19 crisis has had on our lives. For some, it's the struggle with the lack of socialization and comradery. Others are getting an emotional lift by spending time with their families, time that they had been craving while trying to balance jobs, relationships, and children-related responsibilities. However, what could be perceived as quality time has its challenges. This was thrust upon the world with no real time to plan or devise a household schedule prior to diving into this new normal headfirst. Homeschooling meets virtual meetings, virtual meetings meet cooking meals, cooking meals meets being frugal with the grocery spend (with an occasional coveted carry out), and then there is trying to have some semblance of a loving relationship with your partner or spouse. And then there is the all-encompassing fear and stress of the virus and its wide reaching effects on vulnerable family and friends' health and well-being. Will I have a job next week? When will we be able to re-open my business? Can I pay my monthly bills? So many unknowns. Church services are cancelled indefinitely, leaving people feeling lost, alone, and perhaps without a sense of purpose and self-worth. And the sandwich generation is burning it at both ends, simultaneously taking care of parents, children, and extended families.

Two weeks turned into two months, going on four months as of this writing. We're all dealing with the crisis, but it is manifesting itself very differently in each of us. Some people are eating and drinking too much, while others don't have enough to eat. Exercise routines are disrupted.

Mental health is affected day-to-day, which I believe will impact many people for years to come. So, how do we fight this thing and come out a survivor—literally and figuratively?

For me, the Covid Effect has basically culminated into three words: *lack of sleep.* I've always been a light sleeper, but was used to getting a good six to seven hours of fairly solid snoozing per night. No more, my friends! I do my best to get to bed by 11 p.m. For weeks now, I have awakened around two or three in the morning. Sometimes I'm wide-awake. Other days, I can barely keep my eyes open, but my head is spinning with thoughts (good, bad, and ugly) and I can't go back to sleep for the life of me. I don't want to bother my husband, as he needs sleep as bad as I do. (We're both blessed to still be working for a handful of essential businesses that need our services.)

> *"So, rather than fight the head trash, I just throw on the all-too-familiar, two-day-old sweatpants and t-shirt and roust myself out of bed."*

So, rather than fight the head trash, I just throw on the all-too-familiar, two-day-old sweatpants and t-shirt and roust myself out of bed. Optimistically, I usually grab my pillow in hopes of drifting back off at some point. I try to read, do paperwork, and watch TV—anything to bring on the slumber that I so desire. It's a vicious cycle that, frankly, has become a bit of a pattern, or problem, actually. *But it's also become an awakening.* I've seen more sunrises in the last few weeks than I've seen in my entire life. I've watched documentaries and learned about history from shows that I would never venture to watch before. I've had some major cries reflecting on the hardships and pain that the world is experiencing. I've reconnected with friends and family on a deeper level, because I have realized how vitally important those are in my life. I've rediscovered the power of prayer and meditation. There is way too much material "stuff" in my life, and I am slowly ridding myself of that clutter and noise. My closets have never been cleaner or more neatly organized.

> *"People are making time to be kind to one another even though this pandemic is fighting against us with relentless vigor."*

This week particularly, I found myself very inspired by the random acts of kindness and compassion that I've experienced through the TV screen, at the grocery, in the neighborhood or on social media. People are making time to be kind to one another even though this pandemic is fighting against us with relentless vigor. I hope that I can be less selfish and more caring post-Covid. That's my hope for our world.

History has shown tragedy bringing people together many times before, so I'm praying that we all see some human-centric nurturing and caring behaviors emerge from this surreal situation we're living through—day to day.

That said, maybe this insomnia is ultimately going to have some sort of positive impact on my personal life in the long run. It certainly has awakened me for the time being. I admit that I do look forward to an eventual good night's sleep. For now, I am content to sip on my chamomile tea at 3 a.m. from my *Not a Morning Person* mug while I try to stay focused on the positives that may await us in the coming days.

 ## Penny's Palace

My father worked in the banking industry throughout my childhood years. Every year he got two consecutive weeks of vacation, which he would take in the summer. We would spend that time at the family cabin on Barren River Lake. We would spend the days boating, swimming, skiing, canoeing, and of course, fishing.

> *"We learned how to troll for striped bass, cast with lures, drop a trotline, bait a hook with crickets or minnows, and even fish for carp with the nasty smelly dough."*

We learned how to troll for striped bass, cast with lures, drop a trotline, bait a hook with crickets or minnows, and even fish for carp with the nasty smelly dough. We had all different kinds of fishing poles and gear. We each took pride in our tackle boxes and would organize them to the hilt, trying to outdo one another.

In the evenings, my brother, sister, and I would catch lightning bugs, ride our Big Wheels, and play with the other kids staying in the nearby cabins. My parents would just relax on the deck or go down to the boating dock for some peace and quiet that they rarely got to enjoy at home!

Reflecting on these family vacations, it was really the *simplest of times.*

I am a water person. Give me a lake, river, or pond, and my mindset immediately shifts to calm and serene. Give me a BEACH and OCEAN, and I transform into a different person altogether. So, it's no surprise that when my husband and I came upon a tiny beachside town in Florida in the early '90s, it was love at first sight. Beautiful, pink-tinted beaches; tiny cottage homes; beachfront dives; and diners. Bikes were for rent, and there was even a family-owned grocery (which is still operating today)—all within walking distance of each other. Seaside, Florida: our getaway haven to this day.

> **"***We couldn't afford much, but were completely satisfied with our small, two-bedroom space above the one and only coffee shop in the area at that time,* Penny's Palace.**"**

The first time we took vacation time to visit was in 1999. We couldn't afford much, but were completely satisfied with our small, two-bedroom space above the one and only coffee shop in the area at that time, *Penny's Palace.* Much like my times at the lake house, it was all about activities during the day and lazy evenings. We cooked-in at night. The children referred to the one-pot crab broils, hamburgers on the grill, and hearty pasta dishes as "feasts"! We continued to Seaside each year for more than a decade as our children were growing up. Each time, we rented a different cottage. The community grew, but it has kept its quaint specialness that we fell in love with some twenty years prior.

Flash forward to current times. We still frequent Seaside. The older children make it a travel destination with our grandkids. One of our daughters spent her honeymoon there. Each family visit creates new memories that will span generations.

"There's something refreshingly tranquil yet invigorating about enjoying the beauty of God's creations—no matter what the environment."

So, where's your getaway with nature? Do you have an outdoor niche for vacation, long weekend, or just a day off? It might be camping in national parks, mountain venues, biking, fishing at the lake, canoeing on a river, or spending time at a beach community. Or maybe it's just a picnic in the park. There's something refreshingly tranquil yet invigorating about enjoying the beauty of God's creations—no matter what the environment.

When I get caught up in the craziness of the complex lives we all lead, I try to take my mind to where it all started at *Penny's Palace*. I'm not sure that it will ever be as special as with that first Seaside visit—which was the *simplest of times.*

Live for Moments of Joy

Losing a child is referred to as the ultimate tragedy. No matter the circumstance, the pain is unbearable. I experienced a miscarriage when I was four months pregnant with our third child. I didn't talk about it for many years because it was so emotionally raw. It was such a sad experience and an emotionally charged year. It literally changed my outlook on life forever. Yes, that was extremely painful, yet losing a child after *giving birth to the life* that you hoped and prayed for has to be an unimaginable grieving process.

"HER strength has reignited my spirit and energized me to live life for the moments of joy."

I have had family members and close friends lose their sons and daughters to illness, accidents, and senseless acts of violence. Most recently, my friend Debbie lost her son to a tragic car accident as he innocently walked home from a community event. I have tried to be supportive, caring, and reassuring during this horrible time in her life. Somehow, a truth moment was unearthed from talking about her experience of her son's early passing. HER strength has reignited my spirit and energized me to live life for the *moments of joy*. Debbie passed on words of wisdom at one of our recurring morning coffees:

"One of my friends encouraged me to wake up every day with the courage and determination to find a little bit of joy in each day."

So, how does that work? You wake up with this blanket of sadness that you have to somehow get out from under. You need to put two feet on the ground and roust yourself out of bed when every ounce of your body is saying no. You force yourself to get dressed and open up your brain, to go through the motions of surviving another day, suffering the loss of your loved one. Where does having joy in life fit into this grim state of being? For my friend Debbie, it is her relentless faith in God and love for her family.

"God has plans for all of us. The challenge lies in how we embrace those plans."

I pray every day for my children and grandchildren to live safe, healthy, and happy lives. Pretty simple request. God has plans for all of us. The challenge lies in how we embrace those plans. Accept those plans. Live through those plans. Because the pain is real when those unexpected, painful moments happen. You start to really question God: Why me? Why us?

I was talking with Debbie about those questions. Our resolve was simple: We don't have the answers and don't expect to . . . in this lifetime. Our faith drives us to the mindset that we will be reunited with our lost loved ones in eternal life. Families experiencing loss today will survive it, but the experience itself is life-changing.

My renewed outlook on life is to *commit to LIVING*. Life is short. Find gratefulness in every day. Find moments of joy.

To go through the motions of surviving another day suffering the loss of your loved one. Where does *having joy in life fit in* with this grim state of being? For my friend Debbie, it is her

Dear Retta

"So, in the spirit of penning love letters, I want to honor Retta with a brief note to let her know once again how much she meant to me and our family while she was on this earth."

My namesake is my maternal grandmother: Henrietta Whitaker Moore. Her grandma name was "Retta." The fact that we shared the same first name laid the groundwork for the special relationship we bonded since I was a baby. Even though she passed away seventeen years ago, I still find myself wanting to give her a call to tell her about something fantastic that occurred with one of our children or a milestone reached by one of our growing grandkids. By the same token, she was my "go-to" for when I had a struggle or not-so-good news to report. I knew that I could trust her explicitly and could count on her being straight-up honest with her input and/or advice on combating the situation at hand. After I left home for college, our communication continued by phone, sprinkled with diligent letter writing. I would pour my heart and soul into those letters! And she would too. Even though her eyesight diminished over the years, I still could make out her written words on paper and certainly could feel the love expression, whether it was one paragraph or five pages long.

"You were such a great listener. You comforted me through my breakups and supported me through my make ups.

So, in the spirit of penning love letters, I want to honor Retta with a brief note to let her know once again how much she meant to me and our family while she was on this earth. It has ignited a reminder of how her life still impacts us all today.

Dear Retta:

I really miss you. But it is in a good way. Since you went to Heaven, the sadness I felt for the first few years has evolved into gratefulness. Though I still miss those soft hands and that pretty smile, I have been able to translate our time together into beautiful memories that I share with my kids and grandkids. We sure did have a special bond. We sure did share a lot of laughs and the occasional tearjerker moments. We sure didn't take our time for granted. For that, I am so thankful.

You were such a great listener. You comforted me through my breakups and supported me through my make ups. I loved our visits at your house. Just the two of us. The door was always open, even when I would wander in unexpectedly. People often say, "Henrietta, you were named after the right person!" I definitely have some of your "rule the roost" DNA, and I gladly own that trait about me. My family is better off for it.

Speaking of family, you would be so proud of your many grandchildren, great-grandchildren, and great-great grandchildren! We remain a close-knit family even though we don't see each other as often as in the old days growing up. It's hard to believe that you and I saw each other practically every day. What a blessing.

I often find myself wondering, what would Retta say? Although, I think in your eyes I could do no wrong, I always knew that I could tell you anything without being judged. What we enjoyed was unconditional love that went both ways. I am so blessed that I am cultivating that same type of relationship with my grandkids.

Retta, I am so proud to carry your name forward. My only regret is I didn't tell you I loved you nearly enough, but something tells me you didn't need to hear the words. Our love was an unspoken truth that only the two of us could experience. (Actually, I think that you kind of liked having a few secrets of our own!)

Your spirit is with me in everything I do. My love for you is everlasting.

Love and kisses,
Henrietta

Stories Shape Our Reality.
Reality Creates Our Stories.

Life on this earth is a continuous journey. It's my belief that each of us has been put on this earth for a purpose. Discovering that purpose is both daunting and rewarding. Sometimes we excel and reach peak points to celebrate. Sometimes we stumble and struggle to get back up. At times, we go it alone. Other times, we need a hand to hold and heart-mending strength from others to help us along.

We evolve as people through the seasons of life we are experiencing. These experiences manifest themselves into life-lived exerts transcending over time. Toddlers to teens. Students to professionals. Spouses to parents. Grandparents to seniors. Our life stories, birthed from the realities of our personal paths, are in turn what shape the realities that lie ahead. New life learnings and lessons are formed. The circle of life continues.

No doubt there is power in each one of our personal stories. That power might take the form of humor to get a friend through a rough time in her life. Or it might be the story content's relevance that resonates with a work colleague and helps validate his decision-making. A story can evoke emotions that people didn't realize were simmering inside them and needed to be expressed. Storytelling has a way of clarifying an underpinned *AH-HA!* moment. Recalling some of my life's moments in time in short form has been an uplifting experience. Sharing those stories is also a little scary, because I know I'm going to be judged by others on some level. But I am completely OK with opening up about some of my vulnerabilities, because the most powerful stories are the authentic ones. I truly believe that I was meant to do this work—creating conversations that impact people in a positive manner.

That's my story. That's my reality.

Keep sharing!

Embrace & Enjoy – Conversation Starters

Why do we sometimes feel guilty about reaching for our dreams?

Is it OK to live in the clouds instead of getting to the deck?

How can we dig deep and realize moments of joy?

How do we strive for inner peace?

Is our hesitation to venture into new territories self-induced?

Are we taking time to reflect on our AH-HA! moments and take action?

How can you open yourself up to awakenings?

Are we overtly expressing our love for others?

REFLECTIONS

ABOUT THE AUTHOR

Henrietta Pepper was born in Nashville, Tennessee and grew up in a close-knit family in Western Kentucky. She has called Louisville, Kentucky, home since 1985. Henrietta and her husband, Larry Profancik, have been married for thirty years and enjoy every opportunity to spend time with their expanding family. A self-described serial entrepreneur, Henrietta has built a successful career in marketing and advertising spanning more than three decades. After years of working in several renowned advertising and marketing agencies, Henrietta established and operated a successful brand communications firm for fourteen years. While continuing her work as a branding and marketing strategist, Henrietta teaches undergraduate and graduate courses at the University of Louisville's College of Business.

After selling her business in 2018, Henrietta set her sights on writing her first book, a goal that she had tucked away for many years. This work was to be inspired by relatable stories rooted in faith, family, and friends. The stories within these pages rise from experiences that have shaped the course of her life. Henrietta is expanding her storytelling platform to include speaking engagements, uplifting social media content, and other creative means of written expression.

An advocate for further education, Henrietta's own educational background includes dual bachelor degrees from the University of Kentucky and a master's degree from the University of Kentucky-University of Louisville Executive MBA program. A lifelong learner, she has earned accreditation from several leadership training and management programs, including Harvard University.

Aside from spending time with family and friends, Henrietta enjoys holding leadership positions with several organizations and associations supporting women, entrepreneurial endeavors, and underserved communities on local, regional, and national levels. Henrietta's love of music and reading helps guide her spiritual journey as she praises God for her blessings each step of the way.

Made in the USA
Monee, IL
31 October 2020